I0458316

WADZANAI GARWE

STEPPING INTO WADZI: LESSONS FROM MY LIFE

RADICAL SELF-LOVE
AND
RADICAL SELF-COMPASSION

TABLE OF CONTENTS

INTRODUCTION

My journey through life has been marked by many ups and downs, lessons learned, and the development of core beliefs. The title "Stepping Into Wadzi - Lessons from My Life" is a snapshot of my life experiences and lessons, which have stayed with me like a loyal companion, guiding me and sometimes challenging me.

From my earliest days, I faced challenges that shaped who I am today. Growing up, I learned the importance of optimism and how to find hope even in difficult times. My childhood was filled with moments that taught me resilience and the power of a positive outlook. I discovered that even when things seemed tough, there was always a way to find light and move forward.

As I grew older, I encountered situations that required radical acceptance and love. I learned to accept people for who they are and to love without conditions. This was not always easy, but it taught me the importance of compassion, both for others and for myself. These lessons helped me to navigate relationships and understand the value of forgiveness and understanding.

Throughout my life, I have also learned the importance of setting boundaries and letting go of toxicity. There were times when I had to distance myself from negative influences and toxic relationships. This was a crucial step in protecting my well-being and maintaining a healthy, positive environment for myself. Learning to say no and to prioritise my own needs was a significant part of my journey. Balancing different beliefs and perspectives has also been a key part of my life. I have found wisdom in the convergence of science, religion, astrology, and mysticism. Each of these belief systems has offered valuable insights and has shaped my worldview. This balance has allowed me to navigate life's complexities with an open mind and a deep sense of curiosity.

This memoir is not about seeking recognition or acclaim. Instead, it is about speaking my truth and sharing the wisdom I have gained from my experiences. I hope to offer a reflection on the significant events and lessons that have defined my journey. Through this story, I aim to inspire others to reflect on their own lives and embrace the lessons that life offers.

From my earliest memories to the present, each chapter of my life has been a testament to the power of resilience, compassion, and self-discovery. I invite you to join me as I recount the pivotal moments and insights that have shaped who I am today. This is a story of overcoming adversity, embracing love and compassion, and finding beauty in the journey of self-discovery and acceptance.

One of the most important lessons I learned was the importance of radical acceptance. There were times when I had to accept people and situations as they were, without trying to change them. This was particularly challenging when dealing with a specific situation. However, through this experience, I learned that acceptance is a powerful tool for inner peace and harmony.

Another crucial aspect of my journey has been the practice of radical love, loving others without conditions has been a transformative experience. For example, when I had an experience related to love, I learned that love has the power to heal and to bring people closer. This lesson has been a guiding principle in my relationships and interactions with others.

Setting boundaries and letting go of toxicity have also been vital lessons. There were times when I had to make difficult decisions to protect my well-being. For instance, when I had experience related to boundaries, I realised the importance of prioritising my own needs and maintaining a healthy environment. This has been a crucial step in my journey towards self-care and self-respect.

Balancing different beliefs has enriched my understanding of the world. I have found value in both science and spirituality and have learned to appreciate the insights offered by astrology and mysticism. This balance has allowed me to approach life with an open mind and a deep sense of wonder. For example, when I also had experience related to beliefs, I learned that different perspectives could coexist and offer valuable insights.

Through all these experiences, I have come to understand the importance of speaking my truth. Being honest and authentic has been a guiding principle in my life. For instance, when at the age of 50, I declared my HIV-positive state to the world on all my social media platforms, I realised the power of vulnerability and the strength that comes from being true to oneself.

As I reflect on my journey, I am filled with gratitude for the lessons I have learned and the growth I have experienced. This memoir is a celebration of those lessons and a testament to the power of resilience, compassion, and self-discovery. I hope that by sharing my story, I can inspire others to embrace their own journeys and find the beauty in their own experiences.

Join me as I recount the significant events and lessons that have shaped my life. This is a story of overcoming adversity, embracing love and compassion, and finding beauty in the journey of self-discovery and acceptance.

CHAPTER 01

EARLY LIFE AND BEGINNINGS

Birth and Early Childhood

I was born during apartheid in a country called Rhodesia. I am part of the generation that crossed over from Rhodesia to Zimbabwe, which was a time of great change in Zimbabwe. My young adulthood coincided with the early years of my country's independence from colonial rule, a period filled with hope and uncertainty. Zimbabwe had just emerged from years of struggle for freedom. This historic moment greatly influenced my early adult years, shaping the environment in which I grew up and the values that were instilled in me.

My parents were determined to give me the best life they could in Rhodesia. They were optimistic about the future, believing that the end of colonial rule would open new opportunities for the next generation. This optimism was reflected in the way they raised me, teaching me the importance of hard work, perseverance, and maintaining a positive outlook, no matter what challenges came my way.

As a child, I was naturally curious and eager to learn. My parents recognised this and made education a top priority. They understood that in this new era, education was not just a pathway to personal success but also a means of contributing to the nation's growth. They enrolled me in a good school, where I was exposed to a world of knowledge and ideas that fuelled my curiosity even more.

My early childhood was filled with lessons that, though simple, were profound and long-lasting. My parents taught me that life was not always easy, but with determination and a positive attitude, I could overcome any obstacle. They believed in the power of optimism, that even in difficult times, there is always something to be hopeful about. This belief became a cornerstone of my early development, influencing how I approached life's challenges.

Reaching adulthood in post-independence Zimbabwe also meant navigating a society in transition. The country was finding its footing, and so were its people. This environment of change and adaptation mirrored the lessons I was learning at home. Just as Zimbabwe was charting a new course, I was learning to forge my own path, guided by the values my parents instilled in me.

At school, I was encouraged to ask questions, to explore, and to push the boundaries of my understanding. This nurturing environment helped me develop a love for learning that has stayed with me throughout my life.

My parents' emphasis on education was not just about academics; it was also about developing a strong moral character. They taught me the importance of integrity, kindness, and treating others with respect values that have guided me through many of life's challenges.

One of the most important lessons from my early childhood was the value of perseverance. My parents often reminded me that success doesn't come easily, and that the road to achieving my goals would be filled with obstacles. However, they also taught me that these obstacles were not insurmountable. With hard work, determination, and a positive attitude, I could overcome them. This lesson in perseverance was reinforced through countless small experiences in my childhood, whether it was learning to ride a bike, mastering a difficult subject at school, being the only African child in an all-white primary school, or dealing with the typical challenges of growing up.

In addition to perseverance, my parents taught me the importance of adaptability. Zimbabwe, like many newly independent nations, was undergoing significant social and economic changes. My parents knew that being adaptable and open to change was essential for thriving in this new environment. They encouraged me to be flexible in my thinking and to be open to new experiences and ideas. This mindset helped me navigate the complexities of growing up in a rapidly changing society.

My early childhood was also marked by a strong sense of community. I grew up in a family in which my parents had 7 siblings each, so 14 aunts and uncles and the extended family thereof. Zimbabweans were united in their hope for a better future, and this collective optimism was palpable. My parents were deeply connected to our community, and they made sure I understood the importance of contributing to something larger than myself. They involved me in community activities and taught me the value of helping others. I was the eldest female grandchild, so I babysat my siblings and my cousins. This sense of community, combined with the values of hard work and positivity, created a strong foundation for my development.

Another significant aspect of my early years was the balance my parents struck between discipline and encouragement. They set high expectations for me, both academically and personally, but they also provided the support and encouragement I needed to meet those expectations. They celebrated my successes, no matter how small, and used setbacks as opportunities for learning and growth. This balanced approach helped me develop a healthy sense of self-confidence and a belief in my ability to achieve my goals.

As I look back on my birth and early childhood, I realise how much these formative years shaped who I am today. The lessons I learned during this time have been my guiding principles throughout life. The values of hard work, optimism, perseverance, and adaptability, instilled in me by my parents, have helped me navigate life's challenges and seize its opportunities.

These early experiences laid the foundation for the person I have become, and they continue to influence how I approach the world.

Initial Challenges and Formative Experiences

My primary school life began as a mistake. My parents enrolled me in the Regina Mundi Dominican Convent in Gweru (formerly Gwelo). I passed the entrance examination and was one of the Africans who was accepted. At the time, the Dominicans were forward-thinking. They saw the wave of nationalism and understood that independence was coming despite what the colonisers and Rhodesians thought. Thus, they were slowly integrating people of colour into the school system. As a religious educational institution, they had the leeway to do so.

At the time, they were taking in one person of colour at a time. Thus, they would either take an Asian, coloured[1] (mixed race), or African child as the diversity entrant per year. They thought my last name, Garwe, was

---

[1] Coloured is the colloquial term for mixed race children in Zimbabwe

Irish and thus were quite taken aback when an African child showed up to school on the first day of Kindergarten 1 with blue ribbons in her hair and perfectly attired in the school uniform. As I had an acceptance letter, they could not do anything else. I was then transferred to Mutare Convent. In Manicaland Province, unlike Mashonaland Central Province, where the Regina Mundi Dominican convent was located, they had not started accepting children of colour. I was the first African child to attend Mutare Convent. I learnt that children do not see the colour of one's skin. Racism is taught to children; it is not an intrinsic aspect of childhood perception.

When I was in high school, I faced a significant challenge that shaped my understanding of the world and my place in it. I attended the Dominican Convent School, a well-regarded institution in Zimbabwe, known for its strict adherence to academic excellence and discipline. As a student, I was deeply passionate about English. I loved reading, writing, and exploring the depths of literature. My teachers often praised my work, and I was confident in my abilities. Naturally, I expected to be awarded the 'Best English Pupil' prize at the school's annual award ceremony.

However, the reality was quite different. Despite my hard work and consistent performance, the prize was awarded to another student who had not achieved the same level of success in English as I had. I was shocked and confused, unable to understand why my efforts had gone unrecognised.

Shortly before the award ceremony, my parents and I were called into the headmistress's office. The headmistress, a Catholic nun, explained that there had been concerns about awarding the prize to me, an African girl, over a white student. She admitted that it was difficult for the school to justify such an award to the Ministry of Education, given the racial biases that persisted from the colonial era. This was a painful reminder that, even in a newly independent Zimbabwe, the shadows of colonialism still loomed large.

My parents were understandably upset, but they remained composed during the meeting. On our way home, they spoke to me with gentle encouragement. They told me to keep my head up, to continue working hard, and to remember that true recognition often comes in unexpected ways. Their words were comforting, but the experience left a deep mark on me. I felt hurt, disappointed, and unworthy. It was as though my achievements were invisible, dismissed because of the colour of my skin.

Yet, this experience also taught me an invaluable lesson. It showed me the importance of staying positive and believing in myself, even when others doubted me or failed to see my worth. I learned that life is not always fair and that there will be times when our efforts go unnoticed or unappreciated. However, this should never diminish our self-belief or determination to strive for excellence.

This event was a turning point in my life. It strengthened my resolve to pursue my passions and to stand tall in the face of adversity. It also opened my eyes to the realities of the world, where prejudice and bias can overshadow merit and hard work. But instead of letting this experience break my spirit, I chose to let it fuel my drive to succeed.

In the years that followed, I continued to excel in my studies, using the lessons I learned from this incident to guide me. I became more resilient, more determined, and more aware of the challenges that lay ahead. I understood that I would need to work twice as hard to overcome the barriers set before me, but I was ready to face these challenges head-on.

This experience at the Dominican Convent School was one of many formative moments in my life that shaped my character and my outlook on the world. It taught me about the importance of resilience, the power of self-belief, and the need to stay true to oneself in the face of injustice. It also reminded me that while the world may not always be fair, we have the power to rise above these challenges and create our own path to success.

Introduction to Optimism and Resilience

These early experiences shaped who I am today. They taught me that life is not always fair, but I have the strength to overcome challenges. My parents' lessons about optimism stayed with me. They helped me find light in dark times and gave me the courage to keep moving forward. Growing up in the aftermath of colonialism meant that my early life was marked by the complexities of a society in transition. This period was challenging, not just for me personally, but for the entire nation. The values my parents instilled in me became my anchor during these times. They taught me that no matter how difficult things seemed, there was always hope. Optimism wasn't just a feeling; it was a way of life, a conscious choice to see the possibilities beyond the obstacles.

One of the most profound lessons I learned was that optimism isn't about denying reality or pretending that everything is perfect. Instead, it's about facing the truth of a situation with a belief that things can and will get better. This belief kept me anchored, even when the path ahead was uncertain. It allowed me to persevere through the difficult moments, knowing that they were temporary and that better days were ahead.

As I grew older, I encountered more challenges. Whether it was dealing with the lingering effects of colonialism, understanding my identity, or facing personal struggles, I learned that having a positive attitude and believing in myself were key to overcoming these obstacles. My experiences with systemic biases, like the one at the Dominican Convent School, taught me the importance of resilience. I realised that resilience wasn't just about bouncing back from setbacks, but about adapting to change, finding new paths forward, and maintaining hope even in the face of adversity.

Resilience, in many ways, became my greatest strength. It was what kept me grounded when things got tough and what pushed me to keep striving for better. I learned that resilience is built over time, through experiences that challenge us and force us to grow. It's not something we are born with, but something we develop through practice and perseverance.

During my formative years, I also witnessed the power of community and the strength that comes from supporting one another. This collective resilience was especially important in a society recovering from the wounds of colonialism. It was a time when people came together, supporting one another through shared hardships and celebrating each other's successes. This sense of community and shared resilience taught me that I was never truly alone, no matter how difficult things became. It is also a fundamental family trait.

In Shona culture, we do not use the word cousin. Our cousins are our brothers or sisters if they are born of our parents' siblings. Thus, there is no differentiation between my aunt/uncle's child and me in the family. As a collective, we celebrate and mourn together.

The expression 'it takes a village' is an abbreviation of what we, in Chizezuru – the tribe to which I belong, call Hunhu. Hunhu can be loosely translated as showing one's humanness – humanity.

In my personal life, there were moments when I felt overwhelmed by the challenges I faced. But each time, I knew that I was not alone. I came from a people that had overcome several things including migration. The Shona people are Bantu, thus we migrated from West Africa. I did a DNA test, and the results show that I am Broad East African 67% – Luhya, Kenyan; Broad West African 21% – Mende Sierra Leone,

Liberia and Gambia; and Broad Central African 12% – Yoruba, Nigeria, Benin and Togo. So, my blood tells a story. The story of a people who have overcome adversity through adaptation and assimilation. We moved from West Africa and settled in Mashonaland East Province in Zimbabwe. Imagine how many of my ancestors were lost.

In our praise song for our totem Soko, Bvudzijena, Mwenewazvo, we speak of 'Those who came from Guruuswa'. Guruuswa are the grasslands of the African Great Lakes region (East-Central Africa), while James L. Cox writes of an oral tradition that places it in Tanganyika (Tanzania). Guruuswa means 'long grass' or 'tall grass' since it was an area of grassy plains and expansive grassland. Thus, I come from a people who are travellers and who can overcome many challenges. These lessons became my guiding principles, helping me navigate the complexities of life with a sense of hope and determination.

One of the most difficult challenges was understanding and accepting my identity in a world that often tried to define me based on external factors. This journey of self-discovery was not easy, but it was essential. It required me to confront societal expectations and biases, and to embrace who I truly was. Through this process, I learned that true resilience comes from within, from knowing who you are and standing firm in your beliefs, even when the world around you seems to be pushing back.

I was confronted by this sense of identity when I attended the University of Maryland, College Park, United States of America. I naively thought that the African/Black Americans would automatically embrace me as I was African. This was not the case. I threatened their idea of what Africa represented that had been taught to them. I was a middle-class African child, who spoke perfect English with an upper-class British accent and who challenged them intellectually. I was not poor. I did not believe that America was the best nation in the world, and I was competing in their arena and besting them. This was clearly demonstrated in an essay I wrote on 'Cross-dressing in Shakespearean works', and I was able to make the case and get an A+. My Black American professor was taken aback, firstly that I had studied Shakespeare at all coming from Zimbabwe, and secondly that I was conversant with the complex issues of cross-dressing.

I tried to join the National Association for the Advancement of Coloured People (NAACP), an interracial American organisation created to work for the abolition of segregation and discrimination in housing, education, employment, voting, and transportation; to oppose racism; and to ensure African Americans their constitutional rights. I was rejected. I tried to join the college basketball team and I was rejected. I kept facing rejection from people who looked like me. It taught me that we can look alike, but we are not necessarily alike, nor do we share the same values and principles.

Looking back, I see how these early experiences laid the foundation for the person I am today. They taught me that life is a journey filled with both joys and challenges, and that the key to navigating this journey lies in how we respond to these experiences. By embracing optimism and resilience, I was able to find strength in difficult times and to celebrate the beauty and possibilities that life offers. I also found that rejection was not about me as a person. Rejection from a people/community or a system is a sign of fear of the unknown.

As I continue my journey, I carry these lessons with me, knowing that they will continue to guide and inspire me. Optimism and resilience are not just concepts; they are ways of living and choices we make every day to keep moving forward, no matter what life throws our way. These qualities have become the cornerstones of my life, and they have helped me to not only survive but to thrive in the face of adversity.

CHAPTER 02

DISCOVERING RADICAL ACCEPTANCE

Key Experiences That Taught You to Accept Others as They Are

As I grew older, I began to encounter situations and people that challenged my perceptions and beliefs. One of the most significant experiences that taught me about radical acceptance happened during high school. I volunteered to work with disabled children at the Jairos Jiri Association for Rehabilitation of the Disabled and Blind. Wikipedia describes the Jairos Jiri Association for Rehabilitation of the Disabled and Blind as a philanthropic organisation set up in 1950 in Bulawayo, Rhodesia (now called Zimbabwe) to support and train disadvantaged people. The founder, Jairos Jiri, using Christian principles, wanted to help individuals who previously had been marginalised and rejected. Initially the association supported arts endeavours and training and set up craft outlets selling tourist souvenirs, such as carvings, paintings, tiles and furniture. In the 1970s, legal representation and affiliate support groups were founded in the United Kingdom (UK). Jairos Jiri Associations now house the disadvantaged, support musical and dance groups, and are a powerful advocate for those who would otherwise have no voice in Zimbabwe. On their website, it states that currently, in 2024, 'the Jairos Jiri Association (JJA) is the largest service provider to people with disabilities and over 4,500 boys, girls, men and women with disabilities are served in their communities every year through Community Based Rehabilitation programmes.'

I was confronted by children with physical disabilities that challenged my aesthetic. I was teaching the children how to swim, and it required patience and adjusting to each child's limitations. I had to find innovative ways to get the children to love the water. I also felt revulsion at times because the limbs would spasm as the children could not always control their motor functions. I had to confront my own natural inclinations and I had to embrace the body in whatever form it came.

The children had amazing souls. They conquered their fear of water, and I felt an overwhelming sense of responsibility because they trusted me so completely. I could not understand how they could put their trust in a 16-year-old who was still trying to figure out the hormonal imbalances and extreme emotions that define the teenage years. The children's eyes used to light up in anticipation when I arrived, and they would cling to me before I left. I received such pure unconditional love from the children. They truly embodied the essence of radical acceptance of their situation and unconditional love. They would share their challenges with disarming honesty, and we learnt to laugh at limbs that didn't work well or that spasmed or were just so atrophied they didn't work. These children helped me perfect my life-saving skills, and I learnt to float like a beached whale.

I learnt tolerance, patience, and innovation because we had to figure out how to swim without certain functional body parts. Some of the children would lash out in frustration, and I learnt that the anger was not necessarily directed at me but at themselves. It taught me not to take people's reactions personally. A lot of people's reactions are fear- or frustration-based. Radical acceptance means that one faces an unchangeable situation and embraces the reality of said situation and works within the parameters of what is possible in the given situation.

Learning from Family Dynamics

Growing up, my family was a blend of different personalities, each with its own quirks and perspectives. My father was a man of strong principles, often set in his ways, while my mother approached life with more flexibility and openness. This dynamic often led to disagreements, but it also provided a rich environment for learning about acceptance.

As a child, I was often caught in the middle, trying to make sense of conflicting views. Over time, I began to realise that both my parents had valid perspectives, and that their differences did not make one right and the other wrong. It also demonstrated the art of compromise and loving and meeting people where they are as opposed to where one would like them to be. This early lesson in accepting the diversity of thought within my own family set the stage for my later understanding of radical acceptance. It taught me that acceptance doesn't mean agreeing with everyone, but rather understanding and respecting their viewpoints.

My father was fat-phobic, and our family life and the way we approached food as a family is coloured by his approach. My dad was on the Atkins diet perpetually, and thus, even today, I distrust carbohydrates. One of my favourite reflections of the food journey with my father is about our shared love of the off-layer hen or the old cock that one has to boil for hours before it softens. We both loved road runner (poulet bicyclette) chicken, as it's colloquially referred to in Zimbabwe. My father and I loved it so much that we took a New Year's challenge that we would eat roadrunner for 365 days. We did, and we loved it. I still love a good roadrunner.

My father's fat phobia did give me a very warped relationship with my body and weight. For my 18th birthday, my father promised me a whole new wardrobe of new clothes if I lost 10 kilograms (kgs). I was not overweight at the time. I was at the peak of my athletic life, playing basketball, hockey and swimming in my high school teams. I was all muscle, and it was impossible for me to lose any more weight. It also resulted in my never seeing myself as beautiful.

This vision of myself as unattractive had started much earlier during my chubby teenage period. When I was 13 or 14, my mum decided that I was old enough to choose my own clothes. Prior to this, my parents bought all my clothes without my input. My father travelled overseas often so he would buy us all beautiful clothes. My mum is a fashionista and could put an outfit together beautifully. Thus, being allowed to choose my own clothes was huge.

I had always loved dungarees, and I went out and bought myself a pair of denim dungarees. My mum asked for a fashion show to see what I had purchased, and I excitedly put on my dungarees and preening walked into the bedroom where my aunt (my mum's youngest sister) and my mum were sitting. My aunt took one look and burst out laughing. I was hurt. I ran out of the room, and to this day, I have never worn a denim dungaree. She apologised to me about 10 years ago; however, that incident defined by body image. It has taken me over 30 years to develop radical acceptance and love for my body.

These experiences have defined for me the complexity of radically accepting that members of the family can inadvertently hurt and traumatise a young soul and yet they also love the person deeply. My aunt is my mentor and confidante as I navigate this complex life, and yet she also caused me to have body image issues.

Family is the first place that I had to navigate and make sense of diametrically opposing views. Family dynamics taught me that two things can be very different and yet both be true. This forms the basis for radical acceptance because one has to accept that two diametrically opposed behaviours can exist and be true in the same moment.

My parents, my aunts and uncles and everyone in my family were just flawed and complex individuals navigating their lives. Sometimes the traumas we experience because of the family are not malicious or ill-intentioned, they are just someone's involuntary reaction (my aunt), or someone's internal struggles and demons (my dad). Both individuals loved and nurtured me in demonstrable ways, and they also caused me trauma. Two radically different views and behaviours existed in the same space and were equally valid.

Encountering Cultural Differences

Another pivotal moment in my journey toward radical acceptance occurred when my parents became the first diplomats post-independence in the Republic of Kenya. My parents opened the first High Commission to Kenya as my father was appointed the first Ambassador to the Republic of Kenya. As Zimbabwe was part of the Commonwealth, the embassy is known as a High Commission, and my father, the Ambassador, was the High Commissioner. This took me to a different country, where I was immersed in a culture that was vastly different from my own. Initially, I felt out of place and even overwhelmed by the unfamiliar customs, language, and social norms.

One of the most challenging aspects was adjusting to the local way of thinking, which often conflicted with my own beliefs.

I was coming from an apartheid mindset.

Keep in mind that Zimbabwe had only been independent for two years at this point, so the country was very young. I had been indoctrinated for 16 of my formative years during apartheid Rhodesia. The common narrative posited 'White/Caucasian excellence' against 'Black/African mediocrity'. Kenya is and was in 1982, an independent African country. My world and everything I had held as truth were challenged. I was now exposed to an African-run country. The business languages were English and Swahili, with Swahili being the language of choice. I had never been in a country where 'the vernacular or native language' was spoken as a badge of honour.

It blew my mind coming from such a negative narrative about African abilities.

I saw African excellence at work from every sphere – political, technical, legal, security, service, and all other walks of life. It truly gave me wings and arguments against 'white privilege'.

Seeing people who look like me – an African girl child, doing something that is traditionally associated with something one never thought possible is powerful. The fact that Africans could determine their own destiny had been anathema to me. I had a built-in imposter syndrome developed through Rhodesian indoctrination. I was excelling academically, socially, and athletically at my school, and yet I was constantly told I was inferior.

Now, I was in a space where Africans were thriving. Africans were decision-makers in every aspect of their lives. It was mind-blowing and self-affirming. I had found the truth, and it gave me wings.

I was also confused because despite Kenya being 20 years old and having gained its independence in 1962, it still suffered from colonial scars and was trying to shake off colonial trauma. They, too, had to prove the reality of 'Black/African excellence'. One such trauma was that Kenyans did not use their African names. When a Kenyan would ask me, 'What is your name?' I answered 'Wadzanai', and they would shake their heads and say, 'No, that's your traditional name, what is your Christian name'. Kenyans are predominately Christian, and they could not understand that my baptismal name and my actual name were the same. They had two names they used – a Christian name, usually from the bible, and their traditional name.

This taught me that as forward-looking, proudly African, and vibrant a society as Kenya was, it also had the shadow side. Kenya was navigating two truths – a legacy of colonial trauma and creating a new democracy. Both are intrinsically true, and yet one aspect was dark and filled with colonial trauma, and the other was unknown and navigating the realities of self-rule.

As the weeks went by, I started to see the beauty in the culture's traditions and values. I learned to appreciate the richness of their customs and the depth of their history. This experience taught me that accepting cultural differences is essential to truly understanding and respecting others.

Friendships That Tested Boundaries

In my early adulthood, I formed a close friendship with someone who had a very different lifestyle and set of values from my own. I lived in the same geographical space, Sakubva township in Mutare, and yet my school life was in the city at the Dominican Convent, which was a private educational institution, while she went to the local public school. My mother tongue is English. My parents wanted me to excel, so they intentionally prioritised speaking to me in English. My friend spoke our actual mother tongue Shona and even more, a dialect called Chimanyika. I understood Chimanyika in a very rudimentary fashion.

My parents were civil servants, my dad was a school inspector, and my mum was a surgical nurse and thus worked in an office and a hospital. Her dad was a gardener, and her mum was a homemaker who sold tomatoes primarily and other agricultural produce from their home. They lived in the staff quarters, known as the 'servants' quarters' at the back of the public school. They had one room, which served as the all-purpose bedroom-cum-living room, and Mum cooked on a primus stove, which is a pressurised-burner kerosene (paraffin) stove. They cooked outside because of the acrid smell of paraffin or in the covered entryway to their one room when it rained or during winter. She had two younger siblings, and they all stayed together in one room.

During Rhodesian times, the Caucasians, wealthier Africans, and public institutions who could afford live-in house help, maids and/or gardeners, built them these one-bedroom, single-occupant dormitory-style rooms with a shared shower-cum-toilet. The bathroom was a pit latrine with an overhanging shower which was shared by the gardener and the maid as each had their separate room. My friend's father was the gardener at the public school, so they lived in the staff quarters behind her school. The headmaster had allowed her dad to live there with his family in one room.

We lived in a three-bedroom house, and I shared a room with my sister, my parents had their own bedroom, and we lived with my aunt, my dad's sister, who was studying and helping my parents take care of my sister and me.

We had a separate lounge-cum-dining room and a kitchen. The only similarities were that we had an external bathroom, which had a separate shower place and a pit latrine. My dad had built a wooden box with a toilet seat over the pit latrine, so we did not squat to use the loo. The racist Rhodesian regime believed that Africans only deserved a hole in the ground/pit latrine to defecate while they built their homes with internal plumbing.

This friend lived life in a way that I initially found difficult to understand and sometimes even disapproved of. I was too young to understand social class, financial challenges, and the economics of institutionalised racism. I did not understand why meat was not part of their diet, and that when my Mum forbade me to eat other people's food, it was not snobbery but an understanding of the economics of the gardener's family versus a two-income middle-class family.

However, our friendship grew stronger because we respected each other's differences. This relationship was a true test of my ability to practise radical acceptance. It required me to let go of judgement and embrace the idea that there is no single 'right' way to live life. Through this friendship, I learned that radical acceptance means loving and respecting people for who they are, not who we want them to be. It was a powerful lesson in empathy and unconditional support.

Professional Challenges and Growth

Radical acceptance also played a significant role in my professional life. In my first job during university, I worked as a retail assistant in a large-size women's store called Women's World in Bethesda, Maryland, USA.

I worked closely with a colleague who had a very different approach to work than I did. Jackie, a beautiful African American, was a bundle of energy and wisdom. She came from inner city Washington D.C. and used to travel two hours to get to work. She was often late, and it used to annoy me at first. My parents were very punctual people, and to this day, being late for a business appointment gives me anxiety. My father always said that not turning up on time for an appointment was a sign of disrespect.

One day, I asked Jackie why she was always late. Jackie lived with her elderly grandmother, who had health challenges. She had walked to Bethesda Mall to look for a job because she had no bus fare. Public transportation in America is not made to serve the public because of the long distances between states, so many people prefer to drive. Jackie could not afford a vehicle, and she wanted to change her circumstances. Inner city D.C. is where many of the poor live. Bethesda is where affluent people live. Jackie wanted to become affluent, and she worked out that it was better to do so by hanging out in places where rich people lived.

I was Jackie's introduction to African culture, and she was my introduction to inner-city African Americans. When we first met, we both had huge misconceptions about each other. I was smarting from being rejected by the Black/African American community at college, and Jackie's perception of Africa was that we were primitive. We circled and tolerated each other for a few weeks barely civil. The turning point came after the conversation about her tardiness. My natural curiosity and love of diverse stories led me to drive Jackie home and meet her family. She also met my parents. At this time, my father was Ambassador from Zimbabwe to the USA. Once Jackie met my elegant mother, who is an amazing fashion icon, her whole style changed. When I first met her, she used a lot of makeup and wore 'loud' clothes. Her dress style was obnoxious. I did not even realise the profound effect meeting an African family had on Jackie until I was reflecting on our friendship. Jackie started to dress in a classic understated elegant style. She went from glitter to understated elegance. She embraced her natural beauty and stopped plastering her face with makeup. The transformation was incredible. She also started studying for her high school certificate. She also met her partner, a lovely and very shy white boy from Virginia.

One incident that I will never forget is the day one of our clients brought a gramophone into the store. Our store catered to wealthy Caucasian women of ample girth. We were their only interaction with 'people of colour', as Bethesda was quite a white place. We intrigued the women, and we were under a microscope. Under the misguided notion that Africa was backward, the gramophone was produced to introduce the African girl to technology. I had only seen pictures of gramophones as they were antiquated, in my opinion. This was the age of long play (LP) and singles. Google defines an LP record, or Long Play, as a vinyl record format that typically contains a full album of single records. We had record players and not gramophones.

Once I understood what the client was trying to teach me, I laughed and explained to her that even Zimbabwe had progressed beyond gramophones. I then wrote to my aunt (we used to send letters via airmail post then) to send pictures of Zimbabwean life. I then brought them into the store and shared them. Jackie could not believe our lifestyle in Zimbabwe. She began to slowly understand that the narrative she had been fed about Africans being uncivilised was wrong. She visibly gained her confidence, and she started going to the library and researching African history. Her poor fiancé became her listening post as she educated herself and him. She asked me for the pictures to take to her grandmother.

My Mum, who had been struggling to adjust to being a lady of leisure, having been a professional working woman all her life, also discovered a passion. She invited the clients from the store and their friends to tea parties at our home, the Zimbabwean embassy residence, and spoke to them about Zimbabwe.

This led to the gramophone lady, as she became known to Jackie and me, taking a safari to Zimbabwe.

Over time, Jackie and I began to value our lived experiences. Her inner-city upbringing brought fresh ideas and creativity to our projects, something I might not have achieved on my own. By accepting our different upbringings and, thus, different work styles, I not only improved our working and personal relationship but also grew as a professional, learning to appreciate the strengths that others bring to the table.

Accepting Yourself

Perhaps the most challenging aspect of radical acceptance is learning to accept yourself. For many years, I struggled with self-criticism, often focusing on my perceived flaws and shortcomings. I believed that I had to be perfect to be worthy of love and respect. This mindset led to a constant battle with myself, one that left me feeling exhausted and unfulfilled.

I am and was a confident person. I was also young, insecure, and unsure of my place in the world. In Zimbabwe, I was othered by my peers because I was an African in a multi-racial school, and I was one of very few. At home, I was othered by my peers because I went to a school where I interacted with white people, and I spoke English without a Shona accent. I sounded upper-class British. At home, I was told 'Wadzi murungu (Wadzi is a white girl)'. My parents put a lot of pressure on me to excel. A failing grade was unacceptable. I also had to excel in sports and music. I played the piano and was an all-rounder in sports.

I had to carve out an identity that was hitherto undefined. Social media did not exist at the time, so I am the pioneer of being a third culture kid. Wikipedia defines third culture kids (TCK) or third culture individuals (TCI) as people who were raised in a culture other than their parents' or the culture of their country of nationality, and also live in a different environment during a significant part of their child development years. They typically are exposed to a greater volume and variety of cultural influences than those who grow up in one particular cultural setting. The term applies to both adults and children, as the term kid refers to the individual's formative or developmental years. However, for clarification, sometimes the term adult third culture kid (ATCK) is used.

TCKs move between cultures before they have had the opportunity to fully develop their personal and cultural identity. The first culture of such individuals refers to the culture of the country from which the parents originated, the second culture refers to the culture in which the family currently resides, and the third culture refers to the distinct cultural ties among all third culture individuals that share no connection to the first two cultures.

I identify with this definition. Even though I spent 16 years in my own country before travelling abroad, I was part of the more Western Caucasian culture than my parents' traditional African upbringing. When my parents became diplomats, I had to make friends and adjust to completely new geographical and cultural situations.

I am a nomad. I belong everywhere and nowhere. I am a chameleon having to hide in plain sight.

The turning point came when I realised that the same principles of acceptance, I applied to others could be extended to myself. I began to practise self-compassion, acknowledging my imperfections and understanding that they were part of what made me human. This shift in perspective was transformative, allowing me to embrace my authentic self and find peace within.

Embracing Diversity in the Broader World

As my understanding of radical acceptance grew, I started to apply it to the broader world around me. I became more aware of social issues and the importance of accepting and advocating for marginalised communities. This awareness led me to become more involved in social justice initiatives, where I worked alongside people from diverse backgrounds and experiences.

I hate injustice. At primary and high school, as a minority, I faced discrimination and hated being stereotyped. I began to realise that stereotypes have a touch of truth, but they lack context. As Zimbabweans, camping is not something we do recreationally because, for the African majority who live in rural areas, camping is their lifestyle. Thus, a camping holiday would not be an escape from reality – it is reality. The same can be said for hiking. Walking long distances in mountainous or rocky terrain is routine for Africans going about their daily lives. It's not something we do for fun. These are broad generalisations.

At school, we faced racism and discrimination. In boarding school, for example, we were told that using Vaseline, a petroleum-based cosmetic, would make the sheets oily and thus difficult to wash. The assertion is ludicrous and racist because Africans largely use Vaseline to stop their skin from getting dry and ashy. Zimbabwe is also a very dry country and thus needed us to apply Vaseline unlike in more humid environments.

Our sheets were not hand-washed but machine-washed thus, the 'oily sheets' argument was spurious.

An article by Kevin Cokley, Ph.D., about 'The politics of Black hair'[2] summarised the way I felt when the way I presented at school was controlled. In fact, most public schools ensured that African girls and boys alike shaved their heads as the most acceptable hairstyle. The paragraphs in the article I refer to go as follows:

'As a discipline, psychology has not explicitly addressed the psychological impact of respectability politics. The closest attempt might be internalised racism, which is when marginalised and oppressed communities internalise racist stereotypes, images, aesthetics, and ideologies by the White dominant society about their racial group. The Africentric psychologist Kobi Kambon labelled it cultural misorientation, characterised by Black people internalising a Eurocentric cultural orientation (e.g., preferring White features and aesthetics over Black features and aesthetics).

'By whatever name it is called, the devaluation and denigration of Black hair by Black people is psychologically damaging. It is the result of years of socialisation that places White aesthetics and the approximation of Whiteness as the cultural standard by which all racial and ethnic groups are compared. While skin colour is understandably the physical characteristic often focused on around discussions of approximation to Whiteness, it is Black hair that is a particularly important source of cultural pride and counter to Whiteness as the standard. In their study of beauty and body image concerns among African American women, Awad and colleagues found that there needed to be a reconceptualisation of

---

[2] https://www.psychologytoday.com/intl/blog/black-psychology-matters/202312/the-politics-of-black-hair

body image for African American women because hair was given more priority over traditional body image concerns that are typically associated with White women.'

I quote this paragraph because, to this day, certain academic institutions in Zimbabwe dictate African hairstyles and refuse to allow boys to sport afros or both sexes to sport dreadlocks. This grated on my last nerve.

In a Catholic school, religious studies were part of the curriculum and having lived experiences of discrimination and racism, I questioned God. My questions irked the nuns. I asked, 'If God is all-knowing, how then is our end not pre-destined?' I disrupted every class and was constantly sent to the headmistress. I refused to be bullied into a 'blind faith' position because, in my mind, a deity that gave me an intellect expected me to question everything.

I am and was a born activist.

Experiencing injustice, stigma and discrimination in my formative years reinforced the idea that acceptance is not just about tolerance but about actively embracing and celebrating diversity. It taught me that our differences enrich our communities and that by accepting and supporting each other, we can create a more inclusive and compassionate world. It also taught me that understanding cultural contexts, speaking to people and asking questions can help dispel stereotypes and increase understanding and acceptance.

The Role of Radical Acceptance in Personal Growth

Radical acceptance has been a cornerstone of my personal growth. It has allowed me to build deeper, more meaningful relationships and to approach life with an open heart and mind. It has also helped me navigate difficult situations with grace and understanding, allowing me to find peace even in challenging circumstances.

As I write this memoir, I am approaching my 59th birthday. I am so grateful to have been a pioneer from my inception. I was one of the first African children to attend a multi-racial school from Kindergarten 1 to Form 6. I was the first African child to attend Mutare Convent. I pioneered the concept of 3rd culture kids. I am currently one of the first African Women to be the President of the Federation of International Civil Servants' Associations (FICSA).

Through radical acceptance, I've learned that life is not about forcing things to be the way we want them, but about embracing what is and finding beauty in it. This mindset has brought me a sense of inner peace and has allowed me to live more authentically and fully.

Personal Anecdotes and Lessons Learned

Another significant experience that deepened my understanding of radical acceptance took place during my college years. After being rejected by the NAACP, I re-energised the African Students Association (ASA) and became President. Zimbabwe is one of the smaller countries in Southern Africa. I thought all Africans were the same. Boy, was I wrong.

Together with Kameel from Kenya and Kojo from Ghana, I started to navigate African politics. I had to confront every aspect of my Africanness, and I learnt to distinguish Zimbabwean cultural and traditional practices from those of 53 other distinct nations. I also navigated the tribal differences within the nations. It was a journey of wonder and discovery, which has become an intrinsic part of my nature. I actively seek out African artefacts, clothing, food, music, languages and practices. I'm fascinated by how my DNA is broadly West, Central, and

East African as a Bantu, and yet my family and roots are Southern African.

The relationships I built through volunteering at the African Students Association reinforced the importance of radical acceptance. I saw firsthand how accepting others for who they are can create a supportive and nurturing environment where people feel valued and understood. These experiences taught me that acceptance is a powerful tool for building meaningful connections with others. It allows people to be themselves, without fear of judgement or rejection.

Another personal anecdote that highlights the importance of radical acceptance involves an employee named Thelma. Thelma had always been a vibrant and energetic person, but over time, she began to struggle with mental health issues. This was a difficult period for her, and there were times when she experienced manic incidents because she was bipolar. I found it challenging to understand her behaviour, and at first, I wanted to find ways to help or 'fix' what was wrong.

However, I soon realised that what Thema needed wasn't someone to solve her problems, but someone to accept her without judgement. It was a humbling experience to learn that my role as an employer and coach was not to change her or make her better but to simply be there for her. I learned to offer support in the form of listening and being present, without trying to impose my own ideas of what she should do.

Thelma's journey taught me that acceptance is one of the most powerful forms of love and support. It showed me that sometimes, the best way to help someone is to simply accept them as they are, without trying to fix or change them. This lesson has stayed with me and continues to influence how I approach relationships and challenges in my life. It's not always easy to accept people as they are, especially when we care about them and want to see them happy, but I've learned that true acceptance can be incredibly healing.

These experiences with ASA and Thelma have had a profound impact on my understanding of radical acceptance. I have learned that it's about embracing the entirety of a person – their strengths, weaknesses, and everything in between. It's about recognising the inherent worth of every individual and creating space for them to be themselves. This understanding has deeply influenced my interactions with others and has helped me build deeper, more meaningful connections.

Through these experiences, I've come to realise that radical acceptance is not just about how we treat others, but also about how we treat ourselves. Accepting ourselves with all our flaws and imperfections is a crucial part of this journey. Just as we offer empathy and understanding to others, we must also learn to extend that same kindness to ourselves. This process of self-acceptance has been a continuous journey for me, and it has played a significant role in my personal growth and healing.

CHAPTER 03

EMBRACING RADICAL LOVE

Understanding and Practising Radical Love

Embracing radical love was a significant turning point in my life. Radical love goes beyond the conventional understanding of love; it focuses on loving without conditions or expectations. This kind of love means accepting people completely, seeing them for who they are, and loving them despite their flaws and imperfections. My journey toward understanding radical love came through motherhood. I have given birth to two children. My firstborn is a boy named Munyoro Samson (Muni), and my last is a girl Ruvarashe Avery Phillia (Shae). Motherhood is complex, and the terms of reference are overwhelming and powerful. To protect, nurture, discipline, guide, serve, and love unconditionally. This was a new concept for me because I had always believed that love was something that came naturally. I had struggled with the concept of unconditional love when it was challenged by colleagues, family and friends, especially when they were mean or evil.

One of my most impactful experiences with radical love came with motherhood. Motherhood flooded me with such a pure form of love it was unbelievable. I did not always like my children in moments when they were being horrible humans, but I could not stop loving them. My children embody my heart outside my body.

I learnt very quickly as a young mother that a child's personality is evident from infancy. My son is hyper-focused and cannot multitask. He was hyper-focused as a child and, when engaged in an activity, could focus so completely that he would defecate in his pants. If he was playing a Gameboy or with his friends, he would give the activity he was engaged in his complete attention. My son likes to solve problems and he absolutely loves entrepreneurship. He loved a game called SimCity where he created an economic ecosystem. My daughter is not demonstrative and she's very intellectual. She does not like bodily fluids or being touched unnecessarily. I would try to tickle her toes and her feet, and she would just look at me. She was not ticklish. She would fidget after her nappy got soiled as a baby, and she timed her bathroom breaks as a baby. After her last nappy change at night, she would wee in the morning and would start to fidget as soon as her nappy was wet. My daughter is an introvert. She likes doing things alone. She loves small spaces, and she will curl up and read for hours. In many ways, she is as hyper-focused as her brother on absorbing as much knowledge from books as she can.

As a highly demonstrative, touchy-feely Mum, it was difficult coming to understand that my son loved hugs and my daughter wanted minimum contact. They are both ambiverts, which means they have a balance of extrovert and introvert features in their personality, with my son more extroverted and my daughter more introverted.

Over time, through observation, trial and failure and a genuine interest in their well-being, we figured our personalities out. I had to unlearn my pre-existing assumptions and debunk many myths. I also found that there is no 'one size fits all' approach to each child. It was not related to their different sexes either. They were two distinct individuals with their foibles, traits, likes and dislikes, and as their mother, I needed to treat each one and understand their unique personalities. This experience taught me that radical love involves seeing beyond a person's circumstances and loving them for who they are, not for what they have or have not done. It was a profound lesson in understanding that everyone has inherent worth, no matter their situation in life.

Practising radical love also meant confronting my own biases and prejudices. Before becoming a mother, I had unconsciously judged my parents, aunts, and other couples. I had thought that they were lax, overly indulgent, or overly critical. Motherhood humbled me and shattered those preconceived notions. I realised that life is often much more complicated, and people's circumstances are influenced by a myriad of factors beyond their control. This understanding was crucial in helping me develop a more compassionate and non-judgemental approach to others.

Radical love also requires a deep level of empathy. It's about putting yourself in someone else's shoes and trying to feel what they feel. This isn't always easy, especially when someone's experiences are vastly different from your own. But empathy is the bridge that allows you to connect with others on a meaningful level. Through my interactions with my children, I learned that empathy is not just about feeling frustrated, hurt, or trying to control someone; it's about understanding their pain, their joys, and their humanity. It's about recognising the shared human experience and the emotions that bind us all together.

Another important aspect of radical love is the idea of non-attachment. In conventional relationships, love is often tied to expectations – expectations of how the other person should behave, how they should treat us, and what they should give in return. But radical love challenges this notion by encouraging us to love without expecting anything in return. It's about giving love freely, without strings attached, and without trying to change or control the other person. This was a difficult lesson for me to learn, as I had always been taught that relationships were about give and take. But through my experiences, I came to understand that true love is not about what you can get, but about what you can give.

The practice of radical love also extends to self-love. It's about accepting and loving yourself just as you are, with all your flaws and imperfections. For a long time, I struggled with self-acceptance. I was overly critical of myself and felt that I had to meet certain standards to be worthy of love. But as I practised radical love with others, I began to realise that I needed to apply the same principles to myself. I learned that I am deserving of love and kindness, not because of what I do or achieve, but simply because I exist. This realisation was liberating and allowed me to let go of the harsh self-judgement that had been holding me back.

In September 2019, I was hospitalised in 'The Priory', a psychiatric hospital in Woking, Surrey, the United Kingdom. I was suffering from suicidal ideation and complex post-traumatic disorder (CPTSD). I wrote the following journal entry as I recovered from this significant mental illness.

Journal Entry: January 1, 2020 - And Still I Rise

To think that I once gazed upon a knife and attempted to calculate the most efficient way to end my life. I felt compelled to send a message to my baby girl, envisioning the blood spurting from the artery in my neck. I even considered the pattern of blood splatter. The mind is a strange entity. Yet, even amid these thoughts, a rational voice interjected, asserting the inefficiency of dying. The repercussions caused by death far outweigh the relief of embracing that knife and terminating the pain. I have obligations to my children, my loved ones, and my pets.

Suicidal thoughts possess an allure. They seize your thoughts, much like a python winding around you until it squeezes the life out. They whisper enticing words. It will be simpler. It will be over. Why endure this agony?

Haven't you endured enough?

You, girl, can checkmark every "ism" and every conceivable affliction that can and does befall a woman. I am each of them. I've encountered each one.

#MeToo! That's me, Wadzi.

#MeToo!

I am the statistic. My life has been a protest against becoming a statistic, yet here I am, one.

First child syndrome – mine,

date rape – mine,

racism (individual, interpersonal, institutional, and structural) – mine,

sexism – mine,

colourism – mine,

tokenism – mine,

ageism – mine,

ableism – mine,

elitism – mine,

rebellion – mine,

abuse – mine,

disease – mine,

physical disability – mine,

and then,

the strength – mine,

resilience – mine,

survivor – mine,

light – mine,

compassion – mine,

and love mine.

#MeToo!

I am a statistic, and yet I am not. I stand as a marvel of modern science. I am currently held together by antiretrovirals (ARVs), antidepressants, and sleeping pills. Despite this pharmacological cocktail, an inner voice persists. It urges, 'Come on, girl, we must witness the sunrise tomorrow.' It searches for the answer. Why am I still here? Why? I've been on the brink of death multiple times. I've nearly slipped away numerous times, so Why?

I don't possess the answer. Nevertheless, that small voice insists I have a purpose. I hold worth. I carry value. I am not merely a statistic. I must advocate for those concealed in the shadows. I must speak for those paralyzed by fear. I must speak for myself.

So, I greeted this day. It is January 1, 2020, and I continue to breathe. I approach each breath with utmost care because suicide exerts a powerful pull, especially when I'm at my happiest. It's a subtle voice. In every moment, I am presently engaged in a struggle to simply keep breathing. When you encounter me today, give a round of applause. I've made it through today!

Through my experiences, which I listed in detail in my journal entry, I came to see radical love as a powerful force for transformation. It transforms relationships, breaking down barriers, and building deeper connections. It transforms our view of others, allowing us to see their humanity and worth. And it transforms our relationship with ourselves, helping us to embrace who we are with compassion and kindness.

Embracing radical love also means extending this love beyond our immediate circles. It means loving those who are different from us, those who may not share our beliefs or values, and even those who may have hurt us.

This is perhaps the most challenging aspect of radical love, but also the most rewarding. It requires us to let go of resentment, anger, and judgement, and instead, approach others with an open heart and an open mind.

One of the most profound lessons I learned in practising radical love is the importance of forgiveness. Holding onto grudges and resentment only serves to weigh us down and prevent us from experiencing true peace and happiness. Forgiveness is not about condoning the wrongs that have been done to us, but about freeing ourselves from the burden of carrying that hurt. It's about choosing to let go and to love, even when it's difficult. Through my journey, I have found that forgiveness is a key component of radical love, and it is through forgiving others and ourselves that we can truly experience the freedom and joy that love brings.

My marriage taught me that sometimes you can love someone, but they are not good for you. I met my ex-husband when I was 23 and he was 18. I discovered I was HIV-positive just as our relationship became serious in 1992 at the age of 26. I was devastated and understandably confused. I described the relationship in the book *Beyond and Behind the Faces of HIV and AIDS* in my chapter called 'Miracle of Science'. I summarised my relationship with my then-boyfriend, who became my husband, as follows:

'In many ways, my partner and I developed a co-dependence. He became my rescuer, my knight in shining armour, my confidante, my therapist, and I put a lot onto his shoulders. He was 21, and I was the cradle-snatching older woman at 26. Our relationship was toxic from the start because of the co-dependent state we had. We were 'Bonny and Clyde'! In many ways, that is how our relationship played out: Us against the world until we stopped being just US. Our whole marriage was predicated on the fact that he had chosen me, and I could kill him. We were a discordant couple. He was HIV-negative, and I was HIV-positive. We tried using condoms responsibly, but youth, alcohol, and drugs were a recipe for unprotected sex.'

We were young, and we were dealing with an extreme situation. The HIV pandemic swept the world and decimated East and Southern Africa. Our region was a hot spot for the pandemic. One in four Zimbabweans was estimated to be HIV-positive in 1992, when I received the diagnosis, and people were dying daily. We were still very immature, and we had to grow up overnight. We started dating in 1990, married on the 16 April 1994, separated on the 31 August 2014, and divorced on the 3 March

2017. Twenty-seven years – a lifetime lived intensely. As we matured, we grew apart. We did not share the same fundamental values, and it translated into our marriage and parenting styles.

Practising radical love also means being willing to take responsibility for our actions and understand the decisions made at the time and within a specific moment cannot define us.

Hindsight is 20-20 vision, and I have always advocated for, believe in and live, a life of no regrets. The decisions I took at a given moment were contextual. I cannot apply the lens of hindsight, which provides me with a broader perspective of a very narrow time and place. Embracing the philosophy of living a life of no regrets can be difficult and requires courage, but it is an essential part of living a life rooted in radical love. It's about recognising that we are all flawed, and in our connections, we need to exercise empathy and compassion.

As I continue to practise and embrace radical love, I have found that it has transformed my life in ways I never imagined. It has deepened my relationships, brought me a greater sense of peace and fulfilment, and allowed me to see the world through a lens of compassion and understanding. Radical love has taught me that we are all worthy of love and that by loving others without conditions, we can create a more compassionate and just world.

How It Changed Your Perspective and Relationships

Practising radical love fundamentally transformed how I viewed relationships and how I interacted with the people around me. This approach to love, which is centred on giving without expecting anything in return, is my core belief, and it is as essential to my being as breathing, and deeply impacted my connections with family, friends, and even people I didn't know well.

One of the most profound changes was in my relationship with my younger sisters. I have 3 younger sisters who are Chipochedenga (Chipo), 4 years, Nyemudzai (Nyemu), 13 years, and Varaidzo (Vari), 16 years younger than me, respectively. Chipo and I call ourselves the first family as we are closer in years and experiences. We always say our two families – the first family and the second family, Nyemu and Vari, experienced two different sets of parents. When Chipo and I were growing up, our parents were young professionals finding their way in their technical fields and starting a marriage and a family. When the second family came along, our parents were financially, professionally, emotionally, and psychologically more mature. The first family was born prior to independence, and our sisters were 'born free', the term applied to children born after Rhodesia became Zimbabwe. My sister Nyemu was born in 1979, and she was a transitional 'born free'.

In many ways, I am more of a parent to my second family and an older sister. My father died in 1997, and I tried to bridge the gap for my mum. She struggled with becoming widowed and would turn to me for advice. I am a decision-maker and problem-solver, and I find it very difficult when I am asked for advice to restrain from trying to solve the problem. If my proposed solution was not accepted and spurned, I would feel rejected and hurt.

Being an older sister is a complicated dance. I have responsibility without authority. I am asked to advise and try to correct my sisters, but the final decision-maker is my mum and, ultimately, the individual.

As my sisters attained adulthood and started to make their own decisions, I began to realise that I needed to be a non-judgemental sounding board. This change wasn't easy at first. It required patience and a shift in my thinking. Instead of focusing on my need to control and solve problems for my sisters, I started to appreciate that they came to me to vent or to seek advice. They did not necessarily need a solution. I tried to listen to my sisters more and to support their interests, sometimes advocating for them to my mum and even supporting decisions I thought were ill-conceived. This approach helped us to build a stronger, more genuine relationship based on mutual respect and unconditional love. We went from being siblings who barely understood each other to developing a bond that was both deep and enduring.

Another relationship that was transformed by radical love was with a friend who consistently played the victim in the relationship. She took no responsibility for any actions, and everything was someone else's fault. I slowly realised that this was her nature, and I started to define my boundaries and practise radical love. I learnt that there are personality types who can be manipulative and self-serving, and I slowly chose a different path to relationships. I decided to be patient, stating my boundaries clearly and repeating them often. I gave my friend the space she needed, all while letting her know that I was there for her no matter what. This approach was challenging because it required me to set aside my own need for immediate closeness and instead focus on her needs while protecting my sanity.

Over time, we developed a working relationship that embraced our divergent personalities. We carved out the things we enjoyed doing together and learnt to trust each other and respect each other's limitations. She realised that I wasn't going to judge her or abandon her, and this strengthened our friendship. By practising radical love, I learned an important lesson: Sometimes, people need to be loved where they are, not where we want them to be. This has become a guiding principle in all my relationships, helping me to be more compassionate and understanding.

Radical love also changed how I viewed myself. I realised that to love others unconditionally, I first needed to extend that same love and acceptance to myself. This was perhaps the most difficult part of the journey. It meant confronting my own insecurities, acknowledging my flaws, and learning to accept myself as I am. For years, I had been my own harshest critic, always striving for perfection and often falling short. But through the practice of radical love, I began to see that self-compassion was not only important but necessary.

This self-love wasn't about ignoring my faults or pretending to be perfect. Instead, it was about recognising that I was worthy of love and respect, just as I am. This shift in perspective was incredibly liberating. It allowed me to forgive myself for past mistakes and to approach life with a greater sense of peace and confidence. As I learned to love myself more, I found that my relationships with others also improved. I was no longer seeking validation from external sources because I had begun to find it within myself.

The impact of radical love extended beyond my personal relationships and into my community. I am an eternal optimist, and I believe that most people are intrinsically good. I believe that small acts of kindness can and do have a ripple effect, creating a more compassionate and inclusive environment. These experiences reinforce my belief in the power of radical love and show me that it can be a force for good not just in my personal life, but in the wider world as well.

One experience that stands out was my creation of the Edmund Garwe Trust[3] (EGT), a family trust in honour of my late father's prolific life and to honour my journey with HIV and AIDS. EGT's initial goal was to assist child-headed households to embark on economically viable projects in order to combat the disenfranchisement and disinvestment caused by the scourge of HIV/AIDS while living a rights-based life of dignity and self-respect. The goal has expanded, and EGT's goal is currently to promote social public health initiatives and advocate for comprehensive health care for everyone – leaving no one behind.

I formed the trust after completing my postgraduate thesis on 'Violence and Abuse in Child-Headed Households: Causes, Effects, and Remedies a Case Study from Mashonaland East Province, Zimbabwe'[4]. The Trust was formed in 2006 in memory of my father, Edmund Richard Mashoko Garwe, who believed in education as the vehicle for empowerment and independence.

The master's thesis was an exploratory study to find out if child-headed households are susceptible to violence and abuse. The research found that child-headed households are subject to abuse and violence, and one of the major things they lack is time to think and play. The first project of EGT was done through sport in which young girls were provided with life skills, the right to play, and entrepreneurial training. Since then, the Trust has been providing scholarships for child-headed households and is pursuing partnerships in the sphere of social public health with organisations that are aligned with our vision.

This project required a lot of time and emotional energy, and at times, it was overwhelming. However, by approaching it with the mindset of

---

[3] https://edmundgarwetrust.org/
[4] Available on amazon - https://a.co/d/37MgrxA

radical love, I was able to see beyond the immediate challenges and focus on the impact we were making. The gratitude and positive feedback from those we helped were a powerful reminder of why I had chosen this path.

This experience also taught me the importance of empathy and understanding. Many of the people I worked with came from backgrounds very different from my own, and it was easy to judge their circumstances or decisions. But radical love encouraged me to look beyond the surface and to see the humanity in each person. This deepened my sense of connection to others and reinforced the idea that we are all more alike than we are different.

Another aspect of how radical love changed my perspective was in my professional life. I began to apply the principles of radical love to my interactions with colleagues and clients. This meant approaching each situation with empathy, patience, and a genuine desire to understand others' perspectives. In a work environment that often values efficiency and results over human connection, this was a radical shift. But it paid off. I noticed that my relationships with colleagues became more collaborative, and my work became more fulfilling. I was no longer just focused on the end result but on the process and the relationships that were part of that process.

In essence, radical love reshaped every aspect of my life. It taught me to prioritise compassion, understanding, and patience in all my interactions. It helped me to see the value in every person, regardless of our differences, and to approach each relationship with a mindset of giving rather than receiving. This shift in perspective has not only enriched my relationships but has also brought a deeper sense of fulfilment and peace into my life.

As I continue to practise radical love, I am constantly reminded that it is not a destination, but a journey. It is a daily choice to approach life and relationships with an open heart and an open mind. It is about seeing the best in others, and in myself, even when it is difficult. And most importantly, it is about understanding that love, in its truest form, is not about what we can get, but about what we can give. This lesson has transformed my life, and it continues to guide me as I navigate the complexities of human relationships.

CHAPTER 04

COMPASSION FOR SELF

Journey to Self-Compassion and Forgiveness

Learning to be kind to oneself is often harder than being kind to others. My journey to self-compassion was a gradual process that began with the realisation that my inner dialogue was frequently much harsher than anything I would say to someone else. I began to see that this relentless self-criticism was not only unfair but also damaging, trapping me in a cycle of self-doubt, guilt, and anxiety.

One defining moment occurred at work. I was working in my first real job post university. I had landed the job of my dreams, working with refugees as a programme assistant at the United Nations High Commissioner for Refugees. In the chapter 'The Power of an Intrepid African Girl', in the book I co-authored, *You Matter – How Women Reclaiming Their Power Are Changing the World,*[5] I wrote the following:

'My first supervisor was amazing. His name was Godfrey Sabiti, may he rest in peace. He nurtured young professionals, put us in uncomfortable spaces so we could grow to our potential, protected us when we were

---

[5] https://www.amazon.com/author/wadzanaivaleriegarwe

attacked either because of our naiveté, or because we made a mistake, and guided us. I am so glad that my first professional experience gave me the foundation for good leadership skills because our next supervisor was horrible. I was excited to get my first female boss. I welcomed her warmly because I felt honoured that an African woman was in a director position, breaking the glass ceiling. It was a misguided notion. She sabotaged me at every turn. She had delusions of grandeur and was the only one who could shine. She stole reports that I wrote and put her name on them, after telling me to rewrite the report. Imagine being told that one's report is horrible and then seeing the report sent verbatim to headquarters with someone else's name on it. This was my first dose of professional sabotage, gaslighting and undermining my intelligence. I almost fell into depression.'

I then made a significant mistake that had serious consequences because I helped my then-boyfriend land a large procurement contract. He failed to deliver and, in fact, stole the money meant to buy goods and services for refugees. It was a pivotal moment. I was forced to resign, and my awful female boss was ecstatic. She was vindicated, or so she thought. I was devastated, constantly replaying the event in my mind, scrutinising every detail and berating myself for not being perfect. The weight of my own judgement was crushing, and I struggled to forgive myself. I felt as if I had let everyone down, and the guilt seemed unbearable. It was also the moment I attempted my first suicide. I took a whole lot of malaria pills. Luckily my body rejected the attempt, and I regurgitated everything.

It took a long time, but through reflection and support from my father, friends, and mentors, I began to understand that making mistakes is a part of being human. In 'The Power of an Intrepid African Girl' I wrote:

My father taught me my fourth professional and life lesson. Always stand up for yourself! Always state and stand up for what you believe in! You are not a tree, you can move, so leave if a situation is untenable! Do not do toxic situations, even if it means walking away and leaving everything.

I walked into my boss' office, deliberately using the word boss, because she was not a leader, and I confronted her. I said my piece and handed in my letter of resignation. She, of course, smeared my name and created a whole story around how ineffective I was, however, we both knew the truth. I learnt to walk away when a situation became untenable, and I have put on my walking shoes in my career as well as my personal life – leaving employment that did not feed my soul.

This was a profound realisation for me, as it marked the first step toward forgiving myself. I started to see that perfection was an unrealistic expectation, and that holding myself to such a standard was neither fair nor productive.

As I embraced this new understanding, I began to practise self-compassion in small, intentional ways. I allowed myself to take breaks when I felt overwhelmed, recognising that rest was not a luxury but a necessity. I gave myself permission to feel emotions – anger, sadness, frustration – without judging myself for having them. I started to challenge my negative self-talk by asking myself, 'Would I say this to a friend?' If the answer was no, I tried to reframe my thoughts in a more compassionate light. These small acts of kindness toward myself began to shift my perspective. I started to see mistakes not as failures, but as opportunities for growth. This shift didn't happen overnight; it was a slow and sometimes frustrating process. But each small step added up, and over time, I noticed a change in how I viewed myself.

I realised that self-compassion wasn't about excusing my mistakes or ignoring my shortcomings. It was about acknowledging them with kindness and understanding, and using them as lessons to help me grow. I learned that it was okay to not have all the answers and that it was perfectly normal to need help from others. By giving myself permission to be imperfect, I started to release the burden of guilt and began to feel a sense of peace.

Another significant aspect of my journey to self-compassion was learning to forgive myself for past mistakes. There were times in my life when I had been my own worst enemy, holding on to past errors and allowing them to define me. This self-judgement created an inner turmoil that affected my confidence and overall well-being.

Zimbabweans are highly religious and thus actively discourage divorce. In our culture and traditions, apart from the religious aspects, marriage is sacred and a conjoining of two families. It is not an individual pursuit of happiness but a collective good in which, through marriage, one is expanding the bloodline. 'Roora wekumatongo', meaning marry people with similar values so that the bloodline can continue, is the saying. Thus, choosing to love myself enough to divorce was going against culture, tradition, religion, and everything that was held dear in my family. It took me many years to finally make the decision to walk away. The reason it took me such a long time was because I thought I was failing my children, my family, and myself.

Through self-reflection, I realised that holding on to these past mistakes was not serving me. I began to understand that forgiveness, particularly self-forgiveness, was essential for moving forward. It was a way of releasing the past and allowing myself to grow from it rather than be held back by it. This wasn't an easy process; it involved confronting uncomfortable feelings and letting go of the need to be perfect. But as I worked through these feelings, I began to see the power of forgiveness in healing and self-acceptance. I chose radical self-love and radical acceptance.

I also learned that self-compassion was closely linked to self-care. Taking care of my physical, emotional, and mental well-being became a priority. I started to engage in activities that nourished my soul – whether it was spending time in nature, reading a good book, or simply taking a moment to breathe deeply. These acts of self-care were expressions of the compassion I was learning to show myself.

My favourite expression is 'Attend to your basic needs with compassion'. This expression was introduced to me by my therapist. It was life-changing. He helped me put down the load of being my own worst critic to pick up the practice of being my own best friend. When I find myself regressing to the self-critic, I just ask myself, 'What would my best friend say to me in this situation?'

In addition to these personal practices, I sought out communities and support systems that reinforced the importance of self-compassion. Surrounding myself with people who were kind, understanding, and supportive made a huge difference in how I viewed myself. I learned that it was okay to ask for help and to lean on others during difficult times. This support helped me to continue on my journey of self-compassion and to see myself in a more positive light.

As my journey continued, I began to notice how self-compassion transformed my relationships with others. By being kinder to myself, I found that I was also more understanding and compassionate toward those around me.

I became more patient and less judgemental, recognising that everyone is on their own journey and that we all deserve kindness and forgiveness.

One of the most profound lessons I learned was that self-compassion is not a destination but a continual practice. There are still days when I struggle with self-doubt or fall back into old patterns of harsh self-criticism. But now, I have the tools and awareness to catch myself and gently guide myself back to a place of compassion.

Overcoming Internal Struggles and Self-Doubt

Throughout my journey, overcoming internal struggles and self-doubt has been one of the toughest challenges. These doubts often crept in, making me question whether I was truly worthy of compassion or if I was just being too easy on myself. This internal struggle was rooted in a long-held belief that I had to be perfect to be valued. The idea that my worth was tied to my achievements had been ingrained in me for so long that it became a part of my identity.

In my chapter 'Journey with Depression' in the book *Mending the Broken Hearted*, I wrote:

I am alive. I am here. I have a beautiful home near the seaside, and I have contributed to this anthology.

My soul knitted together. My broken heart, stitched back into place. I am whole. I am healed. I am at peace.

I AM HERE!

Do one task a day.

Take one breath at a time.

Attend to your basic needs with compassion.

Wadzanai Valerie Garwe is here.

Wadzanai Valerie Garwe is alive.

I finally figured it out and put my belief in myself and my love of self into practice. I am only human and flawed, and it is okay.

Fear of Failure

One of the most challenging internal battles was dealing with the fear of failure. Each time I faced a new challenge, the fear of not being good enough loomed large. This fear was paralyzing at times, preventing me from taking risks or pursuing new opportunities. It wasn't just about the fear of failing, but the fear of what failure might say about me as a person. Would people think less of me? Would I think less of myself? These thoughts were constant companions, making every decision feel heavier and every mistake more significant.

It was during these times that I had to actively remind myself that self-worth isn't determined by success or failure but by the effort and intent behind my actions. This realisation was crucial, but putting it into practice was a different story. It required me to challenge deeply ingrained beliefs and redefine what success and failure meant to me.

As I reflected on the fear of failure as a parent, I wrote the following in a Facebook post on 12 December 2021:

#conversationswithself I see so many struggle with parental guilt. There is no manual for parenting because it would be impossible to determine how one deals with the different personalities that one brings into the world. I always said to my children their core was determined from the

womb. Both my children are a combination of extrovert and introvert, but they need a lot of time alone. In many ways, they were single children being different sexes, 4 years apart, and the brother going to boarding school from third grade.

So today, I was asked for parenting advice. The first thing I would say is parenting of each child is a Freaking First Time (FFT)! Doesn't matter that you've done it before, but each child is different. My son was malleable he followed rules. He liked structure and thrived in boarding school. My daughter was rebellious and hated structured environments.

The second thing I would say is be careful what you wish for. My overall goal was civic minded, activists with independent minds and thoughts. Both my children will respectfully tell on their view of life and are totally independent. They understand that going against the grain is a hard road; however, they are prepared to take the road in order to achieve their goals.

The third thing to remember is that the template doesn't change. What your parents taught you is the base. So the values you impart come from your background. The variations come with the things you either loved or hated about the original template.

The fourth and final thing is that you will always be the reason for some trauma in your children. It may not be your desire, but you may send them to a school you think is fantastic and yet it's fantastic for you. My daughter told me from the get-go she wanted to be homeschooled. In many ways, I wish I had listened. She did homeschool the last two years of her life and she flourished. She needed a deconstructed environment. I am the reason both children need therapy. Largely absentee, breadwinning parent.

I would say exercise compassion with Self and apologise. Listen. The one thing divorce imposed was active listening. As my children downloaded their pain, anger, fear, love, and happiness, we became a unit. It was painful; however, it taught me to listen.

The hardest part of parenting is allowing your children to fail. As a parent, you want to protect them and make it all better. There comes a time when you have to let the cocoon become a butterfly. It's hard. Watching your child suffer is hard; however, the lessons they will learn from that experience will embolden you.

I hope this helps the young couple who asked. One thing I am grateful for is bringing my children up in countries where I had a village of help. Europe, for young children, is too hard. They need to learn early on in life how to live with, tolerate and love different personalities.

Always remember that your children do not belong to you. They belong to the creator – Musikavanhu. You are the guardian. Love them, be brutally honest with them and do not load them with your expectations. The one thing I refused to do after a certain age, was to make decisions about what they would study. Telling them to follow their passion frustrated them to no end. 'I want to make you proud, Mum' was/is a phrase I hear over and over again. My answer is 'I want you to be happy'! That's it.

As a parent, forgive yourself. Exercise compassion with Self and others. Remember, your children are here for a purpose. Allow them to achieve their highest purpose. And the biggest lesson, especially for single parents – do not sacrifice yourself for your children. You cannot pour from an empty cup. Children learn from the happiness of their parents. Not the constrictions of society. Don't bring them up to play to the gallery of society. Bring them up to exercise their values which may go against those of the society.

Choose your battles wisely. I never fought over hairstyles and fashion. My standard response is and remains it's your hair and your body. I did impose a 16-year age limit for any body piercing, including earrings, and 18 for tattooing. I did not want to be held responsible for any drastic mistakes. Not my circus. Not my monkeys. My battles involved setting basic boundaries. I can hear the groans of my teenage children when I needed to know their friends and their friends' parents numbers. 'We're in Europe now it's different', I would hear being wailed and/or whispered. My standard answer, in these four walls, it's Zimbabwe.

Attend to your basic needs with compassion – ABC.

This post was an ode to me. I was able to write out all my fears of failing as a parent and overcome the fear. I exercised compassion for myself and slowly understood that *we are eternal souls having a human experience.*

Journaling as a Tool for Healing

To overcome my struggles, I began journaling. My journaling happens on my social media platforms and in my personal journals. Writing down my thoughts allowed me to see patterns in my thinking and identify the negative self-talk that was holding me back. It was eye-opening to see how often I criticised myself, even for the smallest things. This awareness was the first step in challenging and changing those thoughts. Journaling became a safe space where I could explore my fears and insecurities without judgement. It was a way to get to the root of my self-doubt and to start the process of healing. As I wrote, I began to understand that these negative thoughts were not truths but narratives I had been telling myself for years. This understanding was empowering, as it gave me the strength to start rewriting those narratives.

Seeking Resources for Self-Compassion

In addition to journaling, I sought out resources like books, podcasts, and talks on self-compassion. These resources provided me with tools and perspectives that helped shift my mindset. I learned that self-compassion is not about being easy on yourself, but about treating yourself with the same kindness and understanding that you would offer to a friend.

One podcast that had a profound impact on me was Brené Brown's *Unlocking Us*. Dr. Brené Brown is a research professor at the University of Houston, where she holds the Huffington Foundation Endowed Chair at the Graduate College of Social Work. Brené has spent the past two decades studying courage, vulnerability, shame, and empathy. Brené's work helped me see that self-compassion involves three main components: self-kindness, common humanity, and mindfulness. Understanding these components helped me to be more forgiving of myself and to see my struggles as part of the shared human experience.

Listening to talks and reading stories of others who had overcome similar struggles also helped me feel less alone. It was reassuring to know that others had faced the same doubts and fears and had found a way to overcome them. This connection to others' experiences gave me hope and motivation to keep working on my own self-compassion.

Shifting from Self-Criticism to Self-Encouragement

Gradually, I began to replace self-criticism with self-encouragement. This shift didn't happen overnight, and it wasn't easy. It took consistent effort and a lot of patience with myself. Whenever I encountered setbacks, instead of berating myself, I would ask, 'What can I learn from this?' or 'How can I support myself through this?' These questions helped me to reframe challenges as opportunities for growth rather than as evidence of my inadequacy.

This shift in thinking made a significant difference in how I approached challenges and setbacks. I started to see them as part of the journey, rather than as signs of failure. This change in perspective allowed me to take more risks and to be more forgiving of myself when things didn't go as planned.

Building Resilience and Self-Worth

By nurturing self-compassion, I found that I could approach life with more courage and less fear. This newfound courage allowed me to take on challenges that I would have previously avoided out of fear of failure. It also gave me the resilience to face difficulties with a kinder heart and a stronger sense of self-worth.

This chapter of my life has been transformative. It has taught me that the most important relationship you have is the one with yourself, and it deserves as much care and compassion as any other. This journey towards self-compassion has not only changed how I view myself but has also improved my relationships with others. By learning to be kinder to myself, I have become more understanding and compassionate towards others as well.

Learning from Setbacks

Setbacks are an inevitable part of life, but how we respond to them can make all the difference. In the past, a setback would have sent me spiralling into self-doubt and self-criticism. I would have questioned my abilities and wondered if I was on the right path. However, as I learned to approach these moments with self-compassion, I began to see setbacks differently. Instead of viewing them as failures, I started to see them as opportunities for growth and learning. This shift in perspective didn't happen overnight, and it wasn't easy. It required a conscious effort to change the way I talked to myself and to challenge the negative thoughts that arose in the face of adversity.

One of the most important lessons I learned from setbacks was the importance of resilience. Resilience is not about never falling down, but about how quickly you can get back up. It's about having the inner strength to keep going, even when things don't go as planned. By approaching setbacks with a mindset of self-compassion, I found that I was able to bounce back more quickly and with a greater sense of purpose.

I broke my ankle on 30 October 2023. In my update on the recovery process, as I journaled on Facebook on 1 February 2024, I wrote:

#conversationswithself I am mentally very well and physically exhausted. Healing is an extreme sport, and broken bones just suck, suck, suck. I have days when I wallow in "woe is me" and then my innate "if not you, then who" comes into play, and I reset and recalibrate. I've been writing, editing, crocheting, and listening to audiobooks, podcasts, and music. Crocheting is a new hobby I have picked up – learnt from YouTube videos. I can crochet anywhere, and it's beautiful. I love crocheting and I must say the solitude and lack of social media makes me happy.

On 30 October 2023, I fell off my bicycle and fractured my ankle. My fracture is so unusual that the orthopaedic surgeon attending to my fracture is on scientific steroids. I have been part of a process where the attending physician is enthralled by my injury. I saw him yesterday, and

*he told me that in his career, I am his second chopart dislocation ever –
and he told me that most orthopaedic surgeons can count the number of
chopart dislocations on one hand in their career ... I'm special. At the
time, he told me this, I was in incredible pain because I had done an
efficiency measure. I chose to put my physiotherapy session before my
doctor's appointment on the same day...*

*I left the house for the first time on Saturday, 27 January, for a social
occasion. I have only left home to attend my check-ups and on Friday
26th, to do my physiotherapy. My sister Chipo Garwe says I am an
overachiever, and I'm beginning to embrace the fact that I am. So,
imagine this – on Friday 26th, I went to my first physiotherapy session in
a wheelchair. I was not walking. In the session, I stood on the foot and
applied pressure, rocking from side to side, stepping and lifting the right
okay leg. I was exhausted after the session. The only thing I was happy to
do was squats. I love squats. However, these squats were special. He, my
physiotherapist (cute as a button), put two scales and I had to squat on
the scales to measure if I was putting equal weight on both knees. Sneaky
physiotherapist.*

*On Saturday, I had a lunch date with two lovely friends... I had asked
them to bring provisions, as I have been doing, and we could cook from
home. Shae was having none of it. She read me the riot act and availed
her services to come to lunch with us at our favourite restaurant, which
is flat. So, I breathed deeply and decided it was time. Time to throw off
the mantle of fear and venture into the world. So, I was wheeled out to the
car in my wheelchair, and I then walked into the restaurant on crutches.
I can liken this event to the child taking their first step. That sense of
wonder. I was amazed that I could put my weight on my foot and walk. It
was both exhilarating and painful.*

So, having now 'walked' on Tuesday, I tackled the stairs to go to have my shower.

Generally, I would sit on a step and use my hands as a lever to take me up the stairs without putting any weight on my foot... I went up and down two flights of stairs.

So, having placed pressure on the foot on Friday, walked into a restaurant on Saturday, gone up the stairs on Tuesday, I foolhardily decided that I could do both a physiotherapy session and do my doctor after. That was highly ill-advised.

As I said – overachiever. There I was on Wednesday morning at 08:15 with an outside (sic) temperature reading at 1 degree Celsius on my way to the physiotherapist. I had graduated from crutches to a walker because I'm too tall for crutches, and I feel completely unsafe on crutches. A walker is more stable and easier for me to manoeuvre. So, there I was, walking my way into the physiotherapy and doing exercises. I was exhausted after, but I recovered in the car on my way to the hospital for my appointment. In the hospital, I went for my X-ray and then to the doctor's room. By the time I got to the doctor, I was in extreme pain. I was done with walking and eyed wheelchairs with envy.

As I entered the doctor's room, I told him I was in incredible pain, and these orthopaedic surgeons are so matter of fact. 'Of course, you are,' he said. 'You had a huge trauma!' Then, he explained how rare my fracture was and how I should expect some level of pain for life. He also explained that the pain I was currently experiencing was caused by the fact that I also needed to develop sufficient bone density and the bone needed to regenerate. He also cautioned that I might need a further operation to insert a pin, should the pain remain unbearable.

Broken bones are an extreme sport. This injury has taught me so much about really taking time to heal. I will definitely not work on efficiency in terms of combined appointments, but efficacy in terms of my overall well-being. I need to be mindful of managing my pain and achieving a sustained state of wellness.

Staying off social media has helped declutter my mind in so many ways. I can breathe without being drawn into the next big event. Being off WhatsApp has truly saved my sanity. I am not commenting on something I have no business being in or starting dramas and battles that I have no business starting because I don't have the platform.

The devil makes work for idle hands.

My hands have been involved in creative pursuits, and yesterday, I got my first order for a crochet shawl. Go figure. I have a hobby I can monetise when I retire – multiple streams of income, right?

So Wadzi is doing good. 2024 has started well. I still have a ways to go in terms of getting to a sustained state of wellness but the journey of a thousand miles begins with the first step, literally.

This post encapsulates my journey with self-compassion, self-love, forgiveness of imperfections and resilience.

Embracing Imperfection

Another important aspect of overcoming internal struggles and self-doubt was learning to embrace imperfection. For so long, I had held myself to impossibly high standards, believing that anything less than perfect was not good enough. This mindset was exhausting and unsustainable, and it only fuelled my self-doubt. As I worked on developing self-compassion,

I began to realise that perfection is not the goal. Instead, the goal is to do my best and to be kind to myself, regardless of the outcome. This shift in focus allowed me to let go of the need to be perfect and to embrace my imperfections as part of what makes me human.

I have spoken earlier about my struggle with my body image, which is a lifelong struggle. As I journaled, I wrote on the 12 November 2022:

#30daychallenge As women, we spend a lifetime struggling to understand that however we present – large, small, petite, plus size, housewife, career woman, and the list goes on – one is enough. Social media, magazines, and now we even have men who have made money from our insecurities, telling us how to dress, how to act, and how to be. And yet we were born perfect. Uniquely crafted by the Creator. I was worrying about my weight for health reasons, not aesthetics, it's hard on the knees to have so much bulk, and my beautiful doctor said to me, 'Wadzi, given everything else, a little weight is the least of your problems.' And I was reminded of this when I waved at a colleague going up the stairs, and she rushed over to give me a hug. I told her she looked amazing, and she said not really because she had put on some weight, but she was happy. I said to her she had never looked better, and it was true. Today, I am grateful for being enough right here, right now, at this moment. Wadzanai Valerie Garwe is enough.

I am enough!

Embracing imperfection also meant accepting that I would make mistakes along the way. Rather than seeing these mistakes as failures, I started to view them as opportunities to learn and grow. This mindset shift was incredibly liberating, as it freed me from the constant pressure to be perfect and allowed me to approach life with a greater sense of ease and self-acceptance.

Developing a Support System

Another crucial aspect of overcoming internal struggles and self-doubt was developing a support system. While self-compassion is ultimately about how we treat ourselves, having the support of others can make a big difference in the journey.

I sought out friends, mentors, and therapists who could offer guidance and encouragement when I needed it most. These relationships provided a safe space for me to share my fears and insecurities and to receive the support and reassurance that I sometimes struggled to give myself. Having a support system also helped me to see myself through the eyes of others. When I was caught up in self-doubt, it was helpful to have someone else remind me of my strengths and capabilities. This outside perspective was invaluable in helping me to challenge the negative thoughts that often clouded my judgement.

Celebrating Progress

As I continued on this journey, I realised the importance of celebrating progress, no matter how small. Overcoming internal struggles and self-doubt is not a linear process, and there are often setbacks along the way. However, by acknowledging and celebrating the progress I had made, I was able to stay motivated and focused on my goals. Celebrating progress also meant recognising the effort I was putting into my growth and healing. It was about giving myself credit for the hard work I was doing, even if the results were not immediately visible. This practice of self-recognition helped to reinforce my self-worth and to build confidence in my ability to overcome challenges.

Continuing the Journey

Overcoming internal struggles and self-doubt is an ongoing journey. It requires continuous effort and a commitment to self-compassion. While I have made significant progress, I know that there will always be new challenges and doubts to face. However, I now have the tools and the mindset to approach these challenges with a greater sense of confidence and self-assurance.

This journey has taught me that self-compassion is not a destination but a practice. It's something that needs to be cultivated and nurtured every day. By continuing to practise self-compassion, I am better equipped to handle whatever life throws my way, with a kinder heart and a stronger sense of self-worth.

CHAPTER 05

OVERCOMING ADVERSITY

Major Obstacles and How You Overcame Them

Life is filled with challenges that test our strength and character. These challenges often come in unexpected ways, pushing us to our limits and sometimes even beyond. One of the biggest challenges I faced was a near-fatal car accident in 2003. I almost lost my life. I suffered an even bigger setback when I fell ill with pneumonia after the accident because of my compromised immune system. My CD4 count fell to 4, and I had AIDS.[6]

The financial strain was significant, and the uncertainty of what would come next was overwhelming. During this time, I felt emotionally drained and questioned whether I had the strength to move forward.

I cannot remember anything about the accident. In fact, it was only through hypnosis that I regained memories.

I suffered many other setbacks in life. In my reflections about trauma and adversity, I learnt about the unconscious vows that one makes to oneself

---

[6]The CD4 count normal range is 500 to 1500 cell/mm^3. If a patient is left untreated, levels can drop below 200 cells/mm^3, which is one indication for the diagnosis of AIDS

and the power of core and limiting beliefs. Vows are solemn promises, pledges, or personal commitments that we make, and I believe when we suffer trauma or adversity, we unconsciously make vows with and to ourselves to protect ourselves from pain.

Lia Watt's article titled 'What Are Beliefs, Core Beliefs, Limiting Beliefs And Belief Systems?'[7] provides the following definitions:

Core Beliefs, Limiting Beliefs And Belief Systems

A core belief is a belief that is the very essence of who you are and central to your identity. Bringing it into question would mean that you question the core of your being.

A limiting belief is a belief that limits us in some way, prevents us from moving forward and achieving goals and keeps us stagnant and stuck. Maybe you see a dream job and think, 'I am not capable,' or 'I do not have the skills.' Maybe a teacher once said you were bad with numbers, so you do not even try to manage your money. Maybe you got hurt in a relationship and decided you are unlovable.

A system is a set of interconnected elements that are organised in a way to achieve something according to defined rules.

A belief system is a set of mutually supporting beliefs that interconnect and support one another to achieve some sort of goal.

---

[7] https://lizwatt.com/articles/what-are-beliefs/#:~:text=A%20core%20belief%20is%20a,keeps%20us%20stagnant%20and%20stuck.

I believe over time as I suffered adversities, I unconsciously made vows to protect myself. Vows are offshoots of pain and fear.

I wrote the following in a group I was part of about 'the vow of invisibility'.

I have been doing 3 months of hypnosis. One session per month. In the first session, it was to address my fear, which was becoming a phobia, of driving. I discovered that my fear stemmed from the fact that my ex-husband had beaten me up on the day of the accident and staged the accident. Imagine a rage that broke my collarbone, my right arm and broke the passenger window on my face. That's how I got a glass and a cut in my left eye. My stomach heaves just thinking about it. He dragged me along the tarmac. No wonder my mind protected me.

In the second session, I dealt with my vow of invisibility. It came about because it was unsafe to be my authentic self. Each time I showed up, it triggered people, so I became afraid of showing myself. It was about racism. It was about unconscious bias (why do you act so white), and it was about belonging. It was my fear of losing my tribe. Fear of being rejected.

In the third session and it was the most intense, I was finding out why I cannot lose weight. It was to protect me. When I was 12, I went shopping for myself. I bought a pair of dungarees, and I was so proud. My aunt packed out laughing and would not stop. When I was 18 in the States, my Dad said if I lost weight, he would buy me a whole new wardrobe. And after my depression, my ex kept saying how heavy and unhealthy I was. 'Have you looked at how big your stomach is'. So, my weight was a protective power because I had been rejected in my own skin. In the last hypnosis, I was asked where I felt the rejection and what colour it was.

My response, it was the colour of vomit in every single cell in my body. Imagine carrying that emotional and physical weight around.

All this to say, our traumas are a result of several visible and invisible cuts that we consciously and unconsciously absorb. The only way we can heal is to love our own skin wholeheartedly and unreservedly. To step boldly onto the world's stage and declare, 'This is I. Take me as I am. I am beautiful.'

Be you, and the world will adjust.

The turning point came when I realised that the only way to overcome my fears, albeit all brought about through adversity, was to focus on what I could control. At first, each problem seemed insurmountable, and the fear of the unknown consumed me. But instead of letting it paralyze me, I decided to break it down into smaller, manageable steps – 'bite-size bits,' as I call them. After the accident I started by sleeping and resting. Even as I panicked about the finances, I understood that I could not work until I healed. As I got stronger, I reached out to my network and explored consulting opportunities. Taking these small steps helped me regain a sense of control and gave me the momentum I needed to keep moving forward.

During any period of adversity and challenges, I leaned heavily on my loved ones for support. I opened up to my family and close friends about my struggles, which is not easy for me. However, their encouragement and understanding reminded me that I was not alone. They offered advice, helped me see things from different perspectives, and most importantly, provided emotional support that is invaluable. Their presence in my life gave/gives me the strength to continue, even when things seem bleak.

Another thing that helped me deal with numerous adversities was shifting my mindset. Initially, I saw failure and a setback. But over time, I began to view it as an opportunity for growth and self-discovery. I started to see challenges not as insurmountable barriers but as chances to learn and improve. This shift in perspective didn't make the difficulties disappear, but it did empower me to face them head-on. By viewing adversity as an opportunity rather than a defeat,

I felt more capable of handling the situation and finding a new path forward.

One of the most challenging obstacles I faced during my recovery from the accident was dealing with the financial instability that came with losing my source of income. In 2003, I was the breadwinner. Our young family, our children were 9 and 5 respectively, had just completed constructing our family home; we were growing our farming enterprise; and I had left my job at Macpherson Consulting Group in 2002 to embark on my own journey as an independent consultant. I had to learn how to budget more carefully and make difficult decisions about where to cut back. It was a humbling experience, but it taught me the importance of financial responsibility and planning for the unexpected. I set small, achievable financial goals for myself, such as paying off debts and building a savings cushion. Each time I met one of these goals, I felt a sense of accomplishment that motivated me to keep going.

Resilience was another crucial lesson I learned during this time. Resilience is the ability to bounce back from setbacks and keep going, even when things are tough.

I realised that resilience isn't something you're born with; it's something you develop through experience and perseverance. Each time I faced a new challenge, I became a little stronger and more resilient. I learned to view setbacks not as failures but as opportunities to learn and grow.

Another significant obstacle I faced was dealing with the emotional toll of this experience. The uncertainty of not knowing what would happen next weighed heavily on me, and there were days when I felt overwhelmed by anxiety and fear. But I knew that I couldn't let these emotions control me. I started practising mindfulness and meditation, which helped me stay grounded and focused on the present moment. By taking things one day at a time, I was able to manage my emotions and keep moving forward, even when the future seemed uncertain.

Throughout these challenges, I discovered that optimism played a crucial role in overcoming adversity. Maintaining a positive outlook, even when things were difficult, helped me stay motivated. It wasn't about ignoring the reality of the situation but about believing that there was a light at the end of the tunnel. This belief gave me the strength to keep pushing forward, even when progress was slow.

Self-care also became an essential part of my journey. When facing adversity, it's easy to neglect your own needs, but taking care of yourself is crucial. I made a conscious effort to rest, eat well, and do things that brought me joy, even if only for a short time each day. These small acts of self-care helped me maintain my energy and focus, allowing me to keep moving forward.

For example, I started taking daily walks in nature, which provided a much-needed escape from the stress of my situation. I also reconnected with hobbies I had neglected, like reading and listening to music, which allowed me to relax and recharge. These activities, though small, had a big impact on my overall well-being and helped me stay resilient in the face of challenges.

I also spent time with the people I loved. My mum, aunts and uncles, my husband, children and my dogs, cats and farm animals. Cocooning and returning to my safe spaces within the confines of my home and loved ones was incredibly healing.

Overcoming these obstacles also taught me the value of perseverance. There were many times when I wanted to give up, but I knew that I had to keep going. Perseverance isn't about pushing yourself to the point of exhaustion; it's about maintaining steady progress, even when the road is rough. It's about showing up every day and doing the best you can, knowing that each effort brings you closer to your goal.

One particular example of perseverance was when I decided to go back to school to pursue further education in 2007–8. It was a daunting decision, especially given my financial situation, but I knew that it was a necessary step for my personal and professional growth. I was responsible for my family; the farming operation was in its inception and my children were in private school. I needed USD 50,000 to pay for our life: my children's education, investing and maintaining farming operations, paying healthcare insurance and studying.

Balancing work, studies, and personal life was incredibly challenging, and there were moments when I felt like quitting. However, I kept reminding myself of the bigger picture and the long-term benefits of this decision. Each assignment I completed and each exam I passed was a step closer to my goal, and these small victories kept me motivated.

In the end, I was able to overcome the challenges that once seemed insurmountable. The journey wasn't easy, but it was worth it. The struggles I faced helped me grow stronger, more resilient, and more compassionate toward myself and others. I learned that adversity doesn't have to define you – it can shape you into a better, more capable person.

Looking back, I'm grateful for these experiences. They taught me valuable lessons about resilience, optimism, and the importance of support from others. They also showed me that no matter how tough things get, there's always a way forward. It may not be easy, and it may not happen overnight, but with patience, perseverance, and a positive mindset, you can overcome even the greatest obstacles.

One final lesson I learned was the importance of adaptability. Life doesn't always go as planned, and sometimes, the path you thought you were on changes unexpectedly. Being adaptable means being open to new possibilities and willing to adjust your plans as needed. This flexibility allowed me to navigate the twists and turns of my journey without getting stuck or discouraged.

For instance, when I left my job at UNHCR, it coincided with my discovery that I was HIV positive. At 26, I had received what seemed like a death sentence as I was one of the casualties of the pandemic, and I had quit my job. I was also in the throws of a passionate, trauma-bonding and co-dependent relationship with my then-boyfriend, and I was undergoing the most catastrophic situation of my 26 years on earth. Culturally I could not move in with my boyfriend and 'bika mapoto' – live in sin because, as the eldest daughter, I was meant to set the example for my siblings. I was also part of a very conservative, religious, and patriarchal society where I could not disappoint or embarrass my parents or bring shame to the family name.

I decided to border jump, run away with my boyfriend and lose myself in Mozambique. It was impulsive. It was also a way to process my personal demons as I had to face my mortality and incorporate uncertainty as a fundamental part of life. My mini rebellion still aimed to protect all those I loved. I could not disclose my HIV status to my parents as it would have killed them.

This openness to change and extreme risk led me to discover new opportunities that were better suited to my mental state, skills and interests. It was a reminder that sometimes, the obstacles we face can lead us to new and unexpected paths that are ultimately more fulfilling.

These experiences have shaped me into the person I am today, and I'm grateful for the lessons they've taught me. They've shown me that no matter how difficult the journey may be, there's always a way forward. It may require patience, perseverance, and a lot of hard work, but with the right approach, you can overcome any challenge and achieve your goals.

The Role of Optimism and Resilience in Facing Challenges

Staying Positive Through Tough Times

Optimism played a crucial role in helping me navigate through the most challenging periods of my life. It wasn't about pretending that everything was perfect or turning a blind eye to the difficulties I faced. Rather, it was about holding on to the belief that things would eventually improve, even when the path ahead was unclear and overwhelming. This belief became a source of strength, fuelling my determination to keep pushing forward.

One of the key aspects of optimism is the ability to maintain hope, even in the face of adversity. When life presented me with difficult situations, I made a conscious effort to remind myself that hardships were temporary. This mindset helped me avoid the trap of dwelling on negativity, which can often lead to feelings of hopelessness and despair. Instead, I focused on the possibility of a better future, which gave me the energy to persevere.

In addition to providing hope, optimism encouraged me to approach challenges with a problem-solving mindset. Rather than becoming overwhelmed by obstacles, I trained myself to look for potential solutions. This shift in perspective was essential, as it allowed me to take proactive steps towards overcoming the difficulties I encountered. By viewing problems as opportunities for growth and learning, I was able to stay motivated and resilient, even when progress seemed slow.

Resilience, closely tied to optimism, is the ability to bounce back from setbacks and keep moving forward. It's about adapting to change, learning from failures, and maintaining a sense of purpose despite the obstacles in your way. Resilience doesn't mean that you never feel discouraged or downhearted; rather, it means that you find ways to pick yourself up and continue the journey, even when things are tough.

One of the most powerful lessons I learned was that resilience is not a trait you either have or don't have, it's a skill that can be developed and strengthened over time. Each time I faced a challenge, I learned more about my own capacity to endure and grow. These experiences taught me that resilience is built through practice, by facing adversity head-on and choosing to keep going.

During particularly difficult times, I leaned on a few key strategies to cultivate resilience. One of these was focusing on what I could control, rather than getting caught up in what I couldn't. This meant breaking down larger problems into smaller, manageable tasks that I could tackle one at a time. By doing this, I was able to make steady progress, even when the overall situation felt overwhelming.

Another important strategy was seeking support from others. Resilience doesn't mean facing everything alone. I found strength in sharing my struggles with trusted friends and family members, who offered not only advice and encouragement but also a sense of connection and solidarity. Knowing that I wasn't alone in my journey made it easier to stay resilient in the face of challenges.

Practising self-compassion was also vital to maintaining resilience. It's easy to be hard on yourself when things don't go as planned, but I learned that being kind and forgiving towards myself is essential for staying strong. By treating myself with the same understanding and compassion that I would offer to a friend, I was able to maintain a positive outlook and avoid the trap of self-blame.

Optimism and resilience also helped me to reframe the way I viewed setbacks. Instead of seeing them as failures, I began to see them as valuable lessons that could guide me towards future success. This shift in perspective was empowering, as it allowed me to view challenges as stepping stones rather than stumbling blocks. By embracing the idea that every difficulty had something to teach me, I was able to maintain my motivation and continue striving towards my goals.

Another aspect of staying positive was the importance of gratitude. Even during tough times, I made a conscious effort to acknowledge the things in my life that I was thankful for. Whether it was the support of loved ones, a small victory, or simply the ability to keep going, practising gratitude helped me stay focused on the positive aspects of my life. This practice of gratitude not only lifted my spirits but also reinforced my resilience by reminding me of the resources and strengths I already possessed. As I wrote in my gratitude diaries, which are digital gratitude journals of the 4 December 2021:

#gratitudediaries In my culture, we have a saying – kusatenda huroyi – ingratitude is evil. My life is richly blessed.

I always say getting HIV was a blessing. I have lived an authentic life because the grim reaper has been always at my shoulder, forcing me to live a life of integrity.

I always say I am not religious because I am a soul having a human experience. Only a man could create a vengeful God who has a hell. As a mother who gave birth to two children, and those children gestated in my womb for 18 months collectively, I know that as the curator of a human being, there is no way I could wish hell on any of my children. I protect them to the death. There is a line in the Bible that says, 'as above so below'. You make your heaven or hell here on earth. Thus, I live my heaven right here, and it begins with gratitude.

I am blessed to be HIV-positive because I know the state of my health at any given moment, and I am acutely aware of my mortality. I am facilitating a book about HIV survivors, either infected or affected, and the group I formed already has 18 participants, some of whom are strangers... Ras Silas Motse is creating the cover for the book. How can I not be grateful? How can this not be divine? I am thankful.

I am grateful for suffering from mental illness because my depression and suicidal ideation have made me aware of the fragility of the human spirit and the human soul. Imagine that the two major diseases I suffer from are internationally marked in December – 2 days apart. December 1 for HIV awareness and December 3 for people with disabilities. Nothing is coincidental on this earth. Having depression reminds me that every human being deserves compassion. Compassion does not mean that I have to endure toxic behaviour. My compassion for myself means I set boundaries to minimise toxicity.

I begin with compassion for myself because I am my greatest critic. That little voice in my head that used to say, 'You are not good enough' has to be rebuked. I was created perfect as I am. I love artists because they create beauty, or they expose rot. Every one of their creations is unique and sends a message. Every creation – painting, poetry, cinematography, photography, the spoken word, dance, the written word, music – has a message. That message stands alone. No artist brings to life and presents something incomplete.

I am an art piece created by the Creator – Musikavanhu, thus I am complete as I am.

I received a gorgeous present yesterday – an avocado, which had travelled approximately 10,000 km, carried in a purse by a sister I had never met. Imagine someone you have never met gifting you the perfect gift. Picking it out and carrying it lovingly from the Congo, via Paris to Rome. I met Veronique Sainte-Luce yesterday for the first time. She is a fellow author from You Matter. *Our souls immediately recognised each other. I am grateful for the journey that brought us together.*

Another thing I believe is that in every incarnation, one recognises a soul they met in a previous life. Nothing happens by mistake. When I went to Sri Lanka, I walked into a church at Galle Fort. My soul immediately became agitated. I had to leave that space, and as I walked out, I saw dungeons. I had a vision of me in a blue dress tied up in the dungeon. Then we walked past a tree in the fort. I had to sit on the roots of this huge tree. I had a vision of myself in chains – chained to that tree. I had never been to Sri Lanka before, and yet here I was having visions. Then we went to a tree plantation in Ella, and I saw a picture of a slave-owning white woman with a coloured child. I dreamt of three children who were ripped from my arms. Why would I have these visions? Do you know that Roots, *the television(sic) series made me physically sick as a teenager? I would watch it and vomit after. I would relive the scenes in my dreams, and it felt as if it had happened to me. It is a series I only watched once, but I am unable to watch anything that depicts slavery. Because I truly believe in a previous life, I was a slave, and the memory is imprinted on my soul.*

I digress. The point I am making is that there are no coincidences in God's creation. Everything is curated. And if I go back to my motherhood story. I now fully understand when the creator says I give you free will. As a mother I can advise my children however they will do what their heart leads them to do. So, free will is a reality, and we replicate it each time we do something. When we, as parents, designed a home for our children there is no way We could have predicted what our children would do with that asset. The creator gave us this earth but there is no way She could predict what we have done with it.

I met Veronique, and she had loving carried my favourite fruit of all time over 10,000 km. A woman who did not know me, except through virtual interactions, brought me my favourite fruit. How is that possible? Because nothing is coincidental. She was a sister I met in the right space, at the right time, and together, we were destined to bring a message to this earth together with 20 other women (including our beautiful publisher). That is not a coincidence; that is destiny.

Every single one who came to our lunch mini-launch yesterday was a beautiful soul. From complete strangers, we found so many connections.

I met Pier who is going to translate You Matter *into Italian via students who have already offered to do this work gratis. However, more than this, Pier would like me to come and speak to the students about Township Girls, and this will lead to Township Girls being available in Italian. I met Anne, an artist who paints uncomfortable things. Things we would rather stay hidden and not spoken about. How this resonated with African Conversations with Self – the platform we curate with Rumbi Pfende, Gamu Mbofana and Avery. We are ensuring the elephant in the room is acknowledged and spoken about. Follow our podcast on Apple podcasts or Spotify*

https://open.spotify.com/show/3HwC8HneMterua08zUUANT...

https://podcasts.apple.com/.../conversati.../id1592075182...

Subscribe to Patreon if you would like to truly understand how Africans feel living in post-colonial white spaces

https://www.patreon.com/africanconversationswithself. How do you think we feel when an African identifies a genome ✄ now called Omicron – and headlines say it's an African virus and we get travel bans? We need to do better as human beings.

I met an artist, Anne, who depicts these uncomfortable conversations visually. I am grateful.

I have only mentioned 2 of the 11 people who joined the luncheon. Each soul has a story to tell, and we are now connected in a group. Marilena Heinrich, the beautiful sister who deserves special mention, conceived of this project, and it has started a movement. I feel grateful.

I have slowly been dipping my foot into the dating pool. I resisted dating apps. Then Facebook made it easy. Everything is a risk, of course, especially in this world where catfishing is a thing. I had my first real date in 7 years yesterday. It was the most affirming, nurturing, and beautiful way to start dating. An Egyptian cinematographer who showed me his work and explained the history of true African Egypt, not the Arab Egypt we have been historically fed. We met as strangers and ended up as friends. How could I not be grateful for Mahmoud? He did not even flinch when I said I have 2 confessions – 'this is my first date in 7 years, so please be gentle with me, and I need you to know I am HIV+'. Do you know how hard it is to have to face potential rejection because of an illness? He took me gently into a hug and said we will take it slowly. I am grateful.

I am grateful for Luca the taxi driver who drives me to Rome and waits until my business is done. He charges me the fare of coming and going and yet spends 5 or 6 hours in a space, which is not his. He is from Romania, and we met because I needed to go to have my PCR[8] test before I left to go to Zimbabwe earlier this year. He was incredibly kind. He is from Romania, and we shared stories about our mothers – our creators. He also saw his mother this year after several years. I was excited to be going to my mother's arms after 2 years of Covid.

All these connections of souls. Never ever think that what happens to you is coincidental. Your soul dictates these connections. I must say, as I sat at the luncheon table, my two favourite Ethiopian brothers walked by, and

---

[8]Polymerase chain reaction (PCR).
This tests for the presence of the actual virus's genetic material or its fragments as it breaks down. PCR is the most reliable and accurate test for detecting active infection. PCR tests typically take hours to perform, but some are faster.

I was able to have long hugs with them after this year of no physical contact. It was amazing.

I am truly thankful for you! You matter to me.

In moments of doubt, I found solace in the stories of others who had faced similar struggles and overcome them. Reading about or listening to the experiences of people who had triumphed over adversity reminded me that challenges are a universal part of the human experience. These stories served as powerful reminders that it's possible to overcome even the most daunting obstacles with perseverance, hope, and a positive attitude.

Finally, optimism and resilience allowed me to remain open to new possibilities and opportunities, even in the midst of difficulty. Instead of being paralyzed by fear or uncertainty, I embraced the idea that every challenge was an opportunity for growth and transformation. This mindset helped me stay adaptable and open to change, which in turn enabled me to navigate life's ups and downs with greater ease and confidence.

Bouncing Back with Resilience

Resilience has been one of the most critical traits that have helped me navigate life's challenges. It's the ability to recover from setbacks, adapt to change, and keep going despite difficulties. Life, by its very nature, is unpredictable and filled with ups and downs. Resilience isn't about avoiding hardship but about how we respond to it when it inevitably occurs. For me, resilience was about finding ways to cope, adapt, and continue moving forward, even when the path was rough.

When I faced setbacks, my first reaction was often frustration or disappointment. However, I quickly learned that dwelling on these emotions didn't help me move forward. Instead, I focused on adapting to the situation. If one approach didn't work, I would try another. This flexibility in thinking was crucial. It allowed me to see challenges not as insurmountable obstacles but as problems with potential solutions. This mindset shift made a significant difference in how I approached difficulties.

Resilience also taught me the importance of patience. There were times when progress was slow, and it felt like I was taking one step forward and two steps back.

During these moments, I had to remind myself that even small steps forward are still progress. Patience with myself and with the process was key. I learned to trust that with time, things would improve, even if the progress was not immediately visible.

One specific example of this resilience was when I faced a significant personal setback. Since September 2019, I have been in poor health. On 15 April 2023, I wrote:

#mentalhealthawareness Do you ever think, 'It would be easier for everyone if I just died?' That's called suicidal ideation. I have to fight that thought more often than you would ever imagine. I'm tired of being a strong African woman. I'm tired of having pain every time I stand because my Achilles hurts. I'm tired of trying to lose weight against a regime of medication and a host of 'everything would be better for you if you just lost some weight'. Do you honestly think that if it were that easy, I would not do it? I'm not a binge eater. My food has been nutritionally curated for decades. And oh, of course, if you stop drinking, your weight will drop off. Have only been having water, and guess what, no miraculous dropping off. I will not have a gastric belt/sleeve or whatever

that surgery is because I cannot traumatise my poor body to that extent, and I know several people who did it who've gone right back to the weight they had and now have complications because of that operation.

It's exhausting to try and remain sane and upbeat when your whole being just wants to give up. The number of people committing suicide is unprecedented. I watched a Facebook video yesterday where artists between the ages of 27 and 35 killed themselves. We have an epidemic, and we need to pay attention. We have a generation succumbing to drugs, prescription or otherwise. All these are huge red flags.

You never know what someone is going through. Be kind at all times, no matter how exasperating, because one side eye or buckle up could be the last straw for that person, especially if they're holding on by a thread. It's very difficult to find a reason to stay alive when everything in the world is dark. Even the weather seems to have given up. It's cold and rainy. I have a basket of washed laundry that I've been unable to hang out for days because it's pouring rain, cold and grey.

For some reason, Facebook reels have an inordinate amount of videos of Twitch dancing with his wife and children. He looks so vibrant and joyful, and yet he took himself to a hotel room and killed himself.

Depression is real. Every minute of every hour of every day that a person with depression makes it through, the day should be celebrated. I write this in order to say to every single person out there who feels the same way – I see you. I get it. I understand that every breath you take is a huge achievement. I applaud the fact that you're smiling through it, responding to messages, and doing what you can to keep holding on. I truly get it.

Remember, one breath at a time. One task a day. If that task is getting up, or brushing your teeth, or taking a shower, or bringing the laundry in (not even folding it), or just getting through a difficult day – well done. Find the little pockets of joy. Watch Netflix, Amazon Prime, or YouTube, listen to your favourite playlist or chat with a friend. Keep finding the little sliver of joy. I know how hard this journey is. It's a marathon, and sometimes in this marathon just do the best you can. You got this.

Attend to your basic needs with compassion (ABC), boo.

It was a time of deep uncertainty and fear, but I knew that giving up wasn't an option. Instead, I focused on small, manageable steps to improve the situation. Each small success built upon the last, slowly but surely leading to a positive outcome. This experience reinforced the idea that resilience isn't about being unbreakable; it's about being able to bend without breaking.

Learning About My Strength

Through these challenging times, I discovered a lot about my inner strength. Before facing these adversities, I had underestimated my capabilities. I didn't realise how strong I could be until I was put in situations that required me to dig deep and find that strength. This strength didn't come from avoiding challenges but from facing them head-on, even when they scared me. Facing adversity helped me build confidence in my abilities. Each challenge I overcame was proof that I could handle more than I had imagined. This realisation was empowering. It gave me the confidence to face future challenges with the belief that I had the strength to overcome them. It was a profound shift in my mindset, transforming fear and doubt into courage and determination.

Strength, I learned, doesn't always mean being tough or unbreakable. Sometimes, strength is about being vulnerable and knowing when to ask for help. There were times when I needed support from friends and family, and I learned that reaching out for help was a sign of strength, not weakness. This was an important lesson in resilience: Knowing that I didn't have to face challenges alone made me stronger.

Growing Through Challenges

Optimism and resilience didn't just help me overcome challenges; they also allowed me to grow through them. These qualities became essential tools in my life, helping me to face future challenges with confidence and hope. I began to see each obstacle as an opportunity to learn and grow, rather than as a setback.

Optimism played a crucial role in this growth. Even in the darkest moments, maintaining a positive outlook helped me see the potential for learning and improvement. It reminded me that every challenge was a stepping stone to becoming a stronger, wiser, and more compassionate person. This perspective allowed me to approach difficulties with a sense of curiosity rather than fear.

Resilience, on the other hand, provided me with the courage to keep going, even when the path was tough. It gave me the determination to keep trying, no matter how many times I stumbled. This resilience wasn't just about bouncing back from setbacks but also about growing stronger with each challenge. Every time I faced adversity, I gained new insights and skills that I carried with me into the future.

One significant challenge that contributed to my growth was the professional journey I am undertaking. This year I chose to focus on staff representation over my technical work as an economist. I described the transition in a LinkedIn article of 11 March 2024 titled 'Everything Is Political' as follows:

I agree that politics plays a part in everything we do. We negotiate with people's cultures, traditions, socialisation, and agendas. As a technocrat, I could combat some of this political intrigue and agenda jockeying with figures – facts and numbers. I am an economist, thus I could model scenarios and I could look at trends and supply the analysis. Politics, in its truest sense, is a different playing field. Politics involves campaigning and agenda-setting. It involves understanding people's motivations at a very visceral level.

I was the only nominee for the position I had just accepted. I naively thought that I would not have to campaign. I thought I could convince people just by my speech. I learnt key lessons: (i) I am now always in the public eye. (ii) The Wadzi who could show vulnerability and authenticity must find a unique way of doing so. (iii) I will be judged on how I dress, how I walk, and what I do or do not do. (iv) There are no safe spaces anymore except those that I carefully nurture. (v) Everything I write and say needs to be fact-checked, referenced, and proofread because I can and will be quoted, and these quotes may be taken out of context. I need to communicate clearly and effectively, brooking no room for misinterpretation. (vi) There are unexpected allies out there. (vii) Those who present themselves to you may be wolves in sheep's clothing. (viii) Always believe that the intended outcome happens – what is meant to be will be. (ix) People are fundamentally against injustice and unethical behaviour. (x) Staff representatives are conservative people.

A clear example of conservatism is the reason I posted my crochet in this post. I attended the opening day of the council with my crochet. I wanted to be fully present to listen to the speeches and to understand the dynamics of present-day staff representation. I did not want to be scrolling on my phone or checking my emails. The delegates were appalled. A potential President crocheting! The gesture was misinterpreted and misunderstood. The delegates thought it was frivolous and disrespectful to crochet. I thought the delegates would appreciate that I was in pain, so the crochet was helping me to distract myself from the pain and instead concentrate on the speeches made in the august body. Huge miscalculation. Fantastic learning curve.

I am not new to political spaces because my father was a diplomat and then joined politics, so I cannot claim complete naivety. I had just not understood, when I put my hat into the fray, that I was already within the political spaces. I had thought it would begin when I made my campaign speech. It began when I was put forth as a candidate.

As a wise man said to me after I sent my thank you email for the support that led to my election: 'I have learnt that in staff representation, we first and foremost deal with the human being, policy, rules, and culture come second. This means dealing with a lot of good, sad, and ugly. It does drive passion, though!'

I am committed to the cause of staff representation. Trade unionism has never been easy. I am ready for the new role and the new challenges and learnings it will bring. In two years, I will be a vastly different animal.

I was faced with decisions that would have long-lasting impacts on my career and personal life. Rather than letting fear take over, I used optimism to stay focused on the potential positive outcomes. Resilience helped me navigate the uncertainty with patience and persistence, ultimately leading to a rewarding outcome. This experience reinforced the idea that challenges are not just obstacles to be overcome but opportunities for growth and self-discovery.

Using Optimism and Resilience in Everyday Life

The lessons of optimism and resilience are not just for times of great adversity; they are tools that I use every day. Whether I'm facing a major challenge or dealing with the small stresses of daily life, these qualities help me stay grounded and focused. They remind me that no matter what happens, I have the strength and the mindset to handle it.

When I face a new challenge, I remind myself of the lessons I've learned and the strength I've developed over the years. I approach each problem with a mindset focused on finding solutions, rather than being overwhelmed by the difficulty. This optimistic outlook helps me stay positive, even when things are tough. It reminds me that setbacks are temporary and that there is always a way forward.

Resilience, meanwhile, helps me stay calm and focused, even when things don't go as planned. I've learned that setbacks are just part of the journey, and they don't have to define the outcome. By staying flexible and open-minded, I'm able to adapt to changes and keep moving forward, no matter what challenges arise.

In my everyday life, this resilience is evident in how I manage stress and navigate unexpected difficulties. I've learned to take things in stride, to not let small setbacks derail my progress. Instead, I see them as opportunities to reassess, adjust, and continue moving forward. This approach has not only helped me overcome challenges but also led to a more balanced and fulfilling life.

I understand that there are two ways to learn – either through following the advice of people who have walked the path or getting burnt. My way of learning has always been experiential in that I learn on the job, so I get burnt, and this reinforces the lesson. I have been learning about living with a disability after breaking my ankle. It has fundamentally changed me because I must be intentional about what I do. I was in the shower, and I now have a shower stool. I stood up to rinse off, and I had a fleeting thought that, before breaking my ankle, I would never consciously think through the positioning of my feet before getting up from the stool. My family will attest to the fact that I have flung my body all over the place. I would fall into a chair, and my maternal grandmother spent countless hours trying to get me to sit like a lady with my legs closed.

I have learnt that my height and weight make me an outlier. Sofas and chairs are usually too low for me, and as I age, I am conscious about ensuring I do not put my back out. According to Wikipedia, the average Zimbabwean woman is 160.3 cm (5 ft 3 in) and in Italy, 162.5 cm (5 ft 4 in), so furniture is made for the average height of the culture. According to world data the average height overall for Zimbabweans is 170 cm (5 ft 5 in) and Italy 174 cm (5ft 7 in). I am 179 cm (5 ft 9 in). I am outside the normal limits. My parents are/were also around the same height. We are outliers. We did not factor into the way things were made. I digress.

The staff representation position I was elected to in March 2024 is forcing me to learn skills that I do not possess. I must change from being a technocrat into a politician. I am now the holder of an elected position. It is not completely new because I occupied the position of General Secretary of the Association of Professionals in the Food and Agriculture Organisation (AP-in-FAO). However, this is a position that was not full-time, and I spent 50% of my time straddling technocracy and political spaces. I was ill-prepared for the higher stakes of the current position.

This is where the point I am making about experiential learning comes into play. I started with a disability because it is something I have lived with for 21 years. For 20 of those years, the disability was not obvious. I had a road traffic accident in 2003, and it left my right hand disabled. I have severe nerve damage; however, I would never tick the disability box on forms because my hand was functional. I could mask its weakness and sometimes, I would drop things because my hand would just open involuntarily. It was so obscure that my sister forgot. She chastised me for carrying a cup of coffee to my mum without putting it on a tray. In our family, this is akin to a cardinal sin. People should be served on trays. I had to remind her that if I carried a tray, I might drop the coffee cup. I am now fully disabled – needing crutches and wheelchairs, so there is no more masking, and I must navigate a world in which I show up as disabled. I must explore getting orthopaedic shoes and finding ways in which I can navigate spaces that do not accommodate disability as much as they try.

When faced with a difficult work project that seemed overwhelming at first, I used resilience to break the task down into smaller, manageable steps. I stayed optimistic about the outcome, reminding myself of past successes and the skills I had developed. By maintaining a positive and resilient mindset, I was able to complete the project successfully, turning what could have been a stressful situation into a rewarding accomplishment.

CHAPTER 06

SETTING BOUNDARIES AND LETTING GO OF TOXICITY

Learning to Set Boundaries

Setting boundaries is about recognising your limits and ensuring that others respect them. It's about saying 'no' when something isn't right for you or when it demands too much of your time and energy. For a long time, I struggled with this. I didn't want to let anyone down or seem difficult. I believed that saying 'yes' to everything made me a better friend, partner, or employee. But over time, I realised that always saying 'yes' was wearing me out and leaving me with little energy for myself.

Recognising the Need for Boundaries

The first step in setting boundaries was recognising when I felt overwhelmed or uncomfortable. At first, I often ignored these feelings, pushing them aside because I felt obligated to fulfil every request. But these feelings were clear signs that my boundaries were being crossed. They were signals that something wasn't right, and I needed to listen to them.

In my professional life, I often took on the difficult and dangerous post-conflict countries at work because I felt a responsibility towards the people who were emerging from conflict. I think it was because of working with Mozambican refugees that I empathise with people who have been in conflict situations. I often worked in emerging states still struggling with post-conflict issues. In 2012, in one such country, the convoy I was in fatally ran over a 9-year-old girl. It was an accident; however, in such situations, people can get highly emotional and subject the people involved in the accident to mob violence. The villagers threatened to burn the vehicle that ran over the child, so, as is the security practice, we proceeded to try to get to the nearest police station. Approximately 10 km after the incident, we were stopped by a militia, which blocked the road. These turned out to be our guardian angels. The leader of said militia proceeded to provide us with an escort and advised the driver to stop driving.

It was a good call as the driver was in no condition to drive. He had never had an accident in his 30-plus year driving career, and his first accident involved killing a 9-year-old child. The deceased child was part of a nomadic tribe who were helping build the roads. Thus, the camp they had created was temporary. We learnt later that the deceased child's mother, having discovered that her child was gone, slit her stomach and aborted her son. I will never understand how the mother chose this action at her time of greatest grief and can only assume it was extreme grief. Her sister then sent a message ahead to inform the militia, who became our guardian angels. Our guardian angels placed themselves in each vehicle, and we proceeded as proposed to go to the police station to report the accident.

We drove for approximately 20 more kilometres and were overtaken and stopped by an army truck and a minibus. The mother's sister was in the minibus, and she had rounded up the troops – literally. She was understandably hurt and seeking vengeance. The girl child is sacrosanct in the nomadic tribes, as women are the creators and nurturers of the bloodline. The unfortunate driver had inadvertently brought a blood feud onto his and his family's shoulders. As we crossed a small stream and started to ascend, we were blocked by the army truck.

The lead guardian angel then showed why he had insisted on giving us an armed escort. One of the soldiers tried to grab the lead guardian angel's gun because he wanted a life for a life. As the only woman in the vehicle that had run over the child, that life was mine. I was the team leader, and as the guardian angel tussled with the soldier, I tried to message for help. I sent a message to our security focal point and the head of the agency, to no avail. I had to do it discreetly as I did not want to raise the ire of an already irate people being egged on by a very angry and distressed aunt (sister of the deceased mother).

Ultimately, the guardian angel managed to persuade the soldiers to take us to the army camp, which was approximately 10 km away. We proceeded to the camp, where we were asked to get out of the vehicle as it needed to be impounded as evidence. The poor driver was thrown to the ground and kicked mercilessly until the commander, who had watched everything happening, finally brought order and stopped the kicking. A young soldier, barely out of his teens and intoxicated, ordered me, 'a high-class woman,' to remove my prescription spectacles. I assume the fact that the lenses were progressive offended his sensibilities, and he slapped me to emphasise the point. Needless to say, everyone removed their spectacles.

After several hours, I had no idea about the passage of time, we were allowed to leave in the two remaining vehicles.

The thing that I did next was what showed a lack of boundaries. The show needed to go on, and as team leader, I just continued as if nothing had happened. I didn't want to disappoint my colleagues or be seen as uncooperative. But this constant people-pleasing came at a cost. I spent countless late nights finishing tasks, and my stress levels soared. Eventually, I reached a point where I realised that to do my best work and take care of myself, I needed to start saying 'no' to extra responsibilities that I couldn't handle. My mind also shut down. I fell into a deep depression.

The Struggle to Say 'No'

Saying 'no' wasn't easy at first. I worried about how others would react and whether they would see me as selfish or unreliable. This fear often made me hesitate, and I found myself agreeing to things out of guilt rather than genuine willingness. But each time I said 'yes' when I wanted to say 'no,' I felt a bit more drained and a bit less in control of my life.

I realised that my reluctance to say 'no' stemmed from a deep-rooted need to be liked and accepted. I didn't want to disappoint anyone, and I feared rejection. But I learned that by always saying 'yes,' I was not only neglecting my own needs but also allowing others to take advantage of my willingness to help.

Learning to Assert Myself

Learning to assert myself was a gradual process. I started by writing out the rules I live by on 12 December 2021 as follows:

#rulesIliveby

I have been on a journey of self-love and self-actualisation since embarking on my 50th year of birth, and I have developed some rules by which I will live:

1. My money is my money, and I can choose to spend it exactly as I like. It is not a collective good. My contributions to anyone are a privilege, not a right. You may not criticise how I spend it. It's none of your business.

2. Unless I solicit your advice about my children, please hold any comments you have to yourselves. Gossip behind my back if you need to – I don't need a face-to-face.

3. Learn not to be offended and whinge and moan at small and stupid stuff. It's wearying and stressful and will simply bring bad blood. Make triply sure that your grievance is justified – don't just whinge because you can or are having a bad day and think that I'm an easy punching bag.

4. Try to make sure that we all leave each other happier rather than angrier when we see each other. I need positivity more than anything else. Simply being family/friends doesn't automatically mean you make my life better.

5. Trust, respect, and love are earned on all sides. Reciprocity is the basis of every relationship. Don't ask for more than you are prepared to give. It is not my responsibility to make other people happy – everyone is responsible for their own happiness.

6. My choices – whether spiritual, professional, personal... whatever – are mine, especially when I fund them myself. You may not agree but reserve your judgements for yourself. Don't try to force your preferences, values, and beliefs onto me.

7. My animals are part of my family so kindly treat them as such if you would like to inhabit the same space as they do.

These are my boundaries. The next stage of my life is about living in harmony with my environment and being happy.

So in order to achieve this zen state, I have outlined my expectations so there will be no confusion.

I reflected on the many areas in which I lacked boundaries, and which impacted on my social health. I outlined my boundaries and communicated them, in this instance, to the world via social media. I started small. For instance, I began to decline social invitations when I needed time to rest, rather than forcing myself to attend out of obligation. I practised saying 'no' in situations where the stakes were lower, which helped me build confidence for when I needed to set boundaries in more significant areas of my life.

One of the most important lessons I learnt was that it's okay to prioritise my well-being. Saying 'no' didn't make me a bad person; it made me a person who respects and values herself. I also discovered that true friends and supportive colleagues understood and respected my boundaries. They didn't see my 'no' as a rejection of them but as a necessary act of self-care.

Understanding the Impact of Boundaries

As I became more comfortable setting boundaries, I noticed significant changes in my life. I felt less overwhelmed and more in control. I had more time and energy to devote to the things that truly mattered to me. My relationships also improved because I was no longer resentful or exhausted from over-committing.

Setting boundaries also taught me a lot about myself. I began to understand my limits and what I needed to feel balanced and content. I learnt to listen to my feelings and to honour them, rather than pushing them aside in favour of others' expectations.

Navigating Difficult Conversations

One of the challenges of setting boundaries is that it often requires having difficult conversations. These are conversations where you have to clearly state your needs and limits, even when it's uncomfortable. I had to learn how to express my boundaries without feeling guilty or apologetic. This meant being clear and direct, but also respectful and understanding of the other person's perspective.

For example, I had to write a letter of emancipation to my children as I couldn't continue to be their constant emotional support without neglecting my own needs. We had tough conversations after the letter, but they were necessary. I expressed my concerns honestly and explained that while I valued our relationship, I also needed to take care of myself. To my relief, my children understood, and our relationship became healthier because of it.

The letter:

> *Via Duino 18A*
> *Fregene*
> *Fuimicino, 00054*
> *Italy*

08 January 2021

Dear Munyoro and Ruvarashe

Emancipation

I had a conversation with Munyoro this morning and I realised that I have erred. You are no longer children under my care but adults and thus are free to make your own decisions and lead your own lives. You are emancipated. As minor children, my obligations were as follows:

- *To protect you from harm.*

- *To provide you with food, clothing and a place to live.*

- *To financially support you.*

- *To provide safety, supervision, and control.*

- *To provide medical care.*

- *To provide an education.*

I have done all these to the best of my ability. As you are both over 18, which is the Zimbabwean legal age of majority under the Legal Age of Majority Act, 1982, my responsibility ceased as an obligation, and I have chosen to support you as your mother until you are able and capable of earning an income. I will continue to support your endeavours to the best of my abilities and wish you the best going forth.

Your father and I provided you with a home, Plot 2 Running Waters Road, Ruzawi, Marondera, Zimbabwe, and that property was registered jointly in your names from the date of purchase. We improved it by building a house plus several outhouses. This property is yours to do with as you wish. I suggest you work out a shareholding agreement that protects both of you in the event of marriage or death. I suggest you consult a lawyer for this. I would like to state categorically that I do not have, nor do I want, any claim to this property, and I do not want to live on this property. I will visit as and when I can and will enjoy my time with you. In my will, any financial and other assets that may remain at my death, are to be shared equally between the two of you as my children.

I would also like both of you to know that you are under no obligation whatsoever and should not feel any pressure to look after me in my old age. I will find a retirement complex and sort out my life until my death. I have a pension, and I am making investments in which I hope to have a steady income as long as I live.

I have tried to treat both of you equitably and thus have seen both of you through your first degrees. Munyoro has chosen not to undertake a master's but requested a personal loan of USD 16,800 (United States Dollars Sixteen Thousand and Eight Hundred) which is equivalent to 2 years of a master's programme. Up to 31 December 2020, the amount transferred to Munyoro in instalments of USD 700 (United States Dollars Seven Hundred) per month is USD 13,059.55 (United States Dollars Thirteen Thousand and Fifty-Nine Dollars and Fifty-Five Cents). The remaining balance will be paid in instalments of USD 700 until May

2021, which will constitute the total amount. Munyoro will advise me of a repayment plan once he is able to do so, and there is no specific time limit on this.

During your college years, I paid for upkeep, accommodation, and tuition. The amounts are similar as Ruvarashe found a school that was free of tuition but her accommodation amounts to the equivalent of what I paid for Munyoro during his schooling in the UK and subsequently in Zimbabwe.

During his college, Munyoro had a vehicle in his name, and I shall provide Ruvarashe, who would like to invest in property, with the equivalent amount of the vehicle when she graduates. The depreciation value of the Opel when handed over to Munyoro was USD 8000 (United States Dollars Eight Thousand), so Ruvarashe can state what she would request in lieu of vehicles on her graduation.

I apologise for any harm and or pain that I may have caused you as a mother. I am sorry. This was a first-time experience with each one of you, and I am sure I have made many mistakes. Everything I have done was in good faith and done out of love. Any harm or pain caused was not intentional, and I hope you can forgive me.

I love you unconditionally. I wish you to live your best lives. As adults, please take responsibility for your lives henceforth. To this end, Munyoro, as you are now 26, please take care of your medical aid, funeral policy, communication costs, and any other necessities that pertain to you. Ruvarashe will still be under my medical aid until her 25th birthday as catered for by the organisation in which I work.

Love

Wadzanai Valerie Garwe

Balancing Boundaries with Compassion

Setting boundaries doesn't mean shutting people out or being inflexible. It's about finding a balance between being there for others and being there for yourself. I learned that it's possible to set boundaries while still being compassionate and caring.

For instance, instead of immediately saying 'no' to a request, I would take a moment to consider whether I could help without overextending myself. If I couldn't, I would offer an alternative or suggest another way to assist. This approach allowed me to maintain my boundaries while still being supportive.

I learnt in therapy that I needed to move from being a rescuer archetype to a coach. A rescuer archetype is defined as someone who instinctively wants to nurture and protect those in need. Overextending oneself: Rescuers tend to put others' needs before their own, sometimes to the point of neglecting self-care and personal boundaries.

On 12 August 2023, I made the following social media journal:

#conversationswithself From Rescuer to Coach – My brain is a strange thing. Sometimes I don't even know that I'm working through or working out something, and then just like that, my brain will say – that's it, processed, here you go. I'm collaborating on a new book with Mukoma Jossine Abrahams and publisher Itayi Garande. My chapter is titled 'A journey of a tortured mind'. It maps some journal entries I made during the depths of my depression. Writing is my process. Some people paint. Some run. I write. I realised as I reread the journal entries that I was processing my depression.

I use social media as my outlet because it helps to know that someone either resonates or opposes my thought process. So last night, my slightly addled brain from some very lethally alcoholic mojito made by Shae, processed a thought that I'm sharing now. My daughter is special. When she cooks or mixes things, she 'feels it in her spirit,' i.e., she uses no measurements. So, her ancestors decided that a lethal concoction of Bacardi, with a touch of soda water, sugar, mint, and lime, was going to be our drink. We had to use a lot of ice and a hell of a lot more soda.

Anyway, I digress. Back to my musings. Don't shoot me, it's a thought in the process.

I think some people don't want to change their painful reality, by painful reality, I mean a chaotic, crisis-filled, horrendously painful something they're going through because they're 'comfortable' in their pain. I know, I know, it's hard-hitting. I realised, though, that some people's process is downloading their pain and soliciting advice, then taking each piece of advice and going no – that won't work for me.

A person will riposte, and I mean that in the dictionary sense as a quick, clever reply to criticism and justify and say things like 'It's not that simple!' 'No, you're not seeing it properly!' or 'You're wrong!' Then, after collective advice, and this is all well-meant, the person will say, 'But I don't want my life to change,' and there's the honesty. And I translate it to 'I don't want your proposed solutions, they won't work for me.'

We, the advisers, solicited or otherwise, need to understand that that person is not seeking advice but to download. We need to learn to actively listen and just shut the fuck up. It's a huge lesson for me. In fact, it's a light-bulb moment in my growth. I know some of you evolved souls are going 'duh.'

I'm processing this because, in one of my therapy sessions, I realised I was a rescuer. Now according to Google: The rescuer connects their self-worth to being needed and taking care of others. They over-function taking on things they perceive as helpful to their partner or that they think their partner 'needs' to be happy. They have come to believe that their own desires are injurious to others and quickly deny them.

I realised by having this light-bulb moment that I'm healed from my specific rescuer persona, which is a trauma response to pain. There is a thing, when you're going through trauma, called the drama triangle or Karpman's drama triangle.[9] Wikipedia explains the triangle in detail, but the synopsis is that in an unhealthy relationship, we have three protagonists:

The Rescuer*: The Rescuer's line is 'Let me help you.' A classic enabler, the Rescuer feels guilty if they do not go to the rescue, and ultimately becomes angry (and becomes a Persecutor) as their help fails to achieve change.*

The Victim*: seeks to convince themselves and others that they cannot do anything, nothing can be done, and all attempts are futile, despite trying hard. One payoff for this stance is avoiding real change or acknowledgement of their true feelings, which may bring anxiety and risk, while feeling they are doing all they can to escape it.*

The Persecutor (a.k.a. Villain)*: The Persecutor insists, 'It's all your fault.' The Persecutor is controlling, blaming, critical, oppressive, angry, authoritarian, rigid, and superior. But, if blamed in turn, the Persecutor may become defensive and may switch roles to become a Victim if*

---

[9] https://en.m.wikipedia.org/wiki/Karpman_drama_triangle...

attacked forcefully by the Rescuer and/or Victim, in which case the Victim may also switch roles to become a Persecutor.

Before healing, I have defaulted to rescuing people, then playing the victim when my solutions are not taken, or the persecutor. Roles are fluid depending on the circumstances.

Now healing involves self-awareness and, of course, tons of internal and painful analysis and observation with a therapist. Once healed, one becomes part of the empowered dynamic, and I quote from the referenced article:

From Victim to Creator[10] –

You can change your thoughts from 'I can't do this for myself' to 'I believe that I am capable of taking responsibility for my own experience.' Write down clear goals. Consider your strengths.

From Persecutor to Assertive Challenger –

Start with voicing your opinion without blaming others. Practise negotiation to create win-win solutions. Provide constructive criticism and allow others to do the same for you. Apply solid boundaries to situations that do not align with your goals.

From Rescuer/Hero to Coach –

The first step in shifting from being a Rescuer/Hero to a Guide is acknowledging that you are enabling others to remain a Victim instead of providing a person the tools to help themselves. Secondly,

---

[10] *https://deschuteswildernesstherapy.com/the-drama.../*

Rescuers/Heroes tend to put their own needs after everyone else's. The transformation from Rescuer/Hero to Guide is in your belief that people can take care of themselves, and where you are a supportive encourager, not a creator of dependency.

People can take care of themselves, and I can provide my analysis of a situation without getting invested in the outcome.

All this to prove my favourite saying, 'Do you and Be you – the world will adjust.'

Thank you for helping me heal, my Facebook family.

The Ongoing Journey

Setting boundaries is an ongoing journey. It's not something you do once and then forget about. Life is constantly changing, and so are our needs and limits. I've had to adjust my boundaries as my circumstances have evolved. Sometimes this means setting new boundaries, and other times it means reinforcing the ones I've already established.

I've also learned that setting boundaries is not just about protecting myself; it's also about building healthier, more respectful relationships. When others know and respect my boundaries, our interactions are more honest and fulfilling.

Letting Go of Toxicity

Part of setting boundaries involves recognising and letting go of toxic relationships and environments. Toxicity can come in many forms – it could be a friend who constantly drains your energy, a work environment that's overly demanding, or even negative thought patterns that keep you stuck.

Letting go of toxicity was one of the hardest but most liberating aspects of my journey. It meant acknowledging that certain people or situations were no longer serving my well-being and taking steps to distance myself from them.

For example, I had a friend who was always negative and critical. Every interaction left me feeling drained and diminished. I struggled with the decision to distance myself because I cared about this person, but I realised that maintaining the relationship was harming my mental health. I had to cut her out of my life.

I realised that she was not a real friend. The friendship was based on her wants and needs and not on mine. This became very clear around the Coronavirus debate. She neglected to tell me that she was against the COVID-19 vaccinations. I was very vocal and communicated my position on the Coronavirus. I was pro-vaccines, and anyone who was coming into my personal space needed to be vaccinated as I was immunocompromised.

I said it directly to my friend and anyone who chose to listen. When the restrictions against meeting in person were lifted, I had a party. I was very specific about the fact that every person coming to the party should be vaccinated, as we were not going to wear masks. The party was lovely, and we had a good time. This was all around Christmas time, and my friend had been travelling quite a bit. She's a wanderer and hates sitting still. She contracted COVID and sent me a message. I responded that, given that she had the vaccine, she should be fine in a few days.

'I am not vaccinated! I do not believe in the vaccine!' she said. I felt betrayed and extremely angry. She had lied to me. Her response when I asked why she had lied to me was, 'You never asked me. If you had asked,

I would have told you.' I felt as if a bucket of cold water had been poured over my head. I did a type of rewind on all the times I had felt disregarded and unheard in our relationship, and I realised that we did not have a friendship. I also took responsibility for my accommodations in the relationship.

I understood over time that **people know exactly what they are doing until they get exposed!** In Chizezuru, my mother tongue, we have a saying, 'nyadzi dzinokunda rufu,' meaning shame is harder to bear than death.

People do not like it when you set personal limits. They react. They react negatively and try to push back. My friend attacked me. She gaslit me by trying to put the onus on me to ask her when I had shouted from the rooftops about my stance on the COVID vaccinations. I chose nonviolence. I walked away. I blocked and deleted her from my life.

It was a tough conversation, which led to no contact, but it was necessary. I expressed my concerns honestly and explained that while I valued our friendship, I also needed to take care of myself. I walked away because my ex-friend was not prepared to take responsibility for her irresponsible and harmful actions, and she was not prepared to do better.

Letting go of toxic relationships doesn't mean you don't care about the person. It means you care enough about yourself to prioritise your well-being. It's about recognising that you can't change others, but you can change how you respond to them.

Reclaiming Your Life

By setting boundaries and letting go of toxicity, I reclaimed my life. I stopped letting others dictate how I spent my time and energy. I started living in a way that was true to myself, rather than constantly trying to meet others' expectations. This process also helped me rediscover my passions and interests. With more time and energy available, I could focus on the things that brought me joy and fulfilment. I could invest in relationships that were nurturing and positive, rather than draining and toxic.

Setting boundaries and letting go of toxicity is not a one-time event; it's a continuous process of self-reflection and growth. It requires courage and honesty, but the rewards are profound. By respecting your limits and protecting your well-being, you create a life that is balanced, healthy, and true to who you are.

Stories of Letting Go of Toxic Relationships or Situations

Letting go of toxic relationships or situations is never easy, but it's a crucial step towards protecting your well-being and finding peace. I've experienced several instances where I had to make tough decisions to remove myself from unhealthy environments. These experiences taught me a lot about self-respect, courage, and the value of surrounding myself with positive influences.

A Toxic Friendship

One of the first situations I had to walk away from was a friendship that had turned toxic. Initially, this friend and I had a lot in common, and we spent a lot of time together. But over time, I started to notice that our interactions were becoming one-sided. My friend would constantly vent about their problems without ever showing interest in how I was doing. Worse, they often dismissed my feelings or opinions, making me feel small and unimportant. I tried to ignore these red flags because I didn't want to lose the friendship. But as time went on, I realised that this relationship was draining me emotionally.

The turning point came during a conversation where she insulted my family. She tried to create chaos and lies about a situation that she culturally could not understand. She weaponised her white privilege. I have researched white privilege, and the best definition I have found is by Peggy McIntosh in her paper 'White Privilege and Male Privilege: A Personal Account of Coming to See Correspondences Through Work in Women's Studies.' She says, 'I think whites are carefully taught not to recognise white privilege, as males are taught not to recognise male privilege. So I have begun in an untutored way to ask what it is like to have white privilege. This paper is a partial record of my personal observations and not a scholarly analysis. It is based on my daily experiences within my particular circumstances. I have come to see white privilege as an invisible package of unearned assets that I can count on cashing in each day, but about which I was 'meant' to remain oblivious. White privilege is like an invisible weightless knapsack of special provisions, assurances, tools, maps, guides, codebooks, passports, visas, clothes, compass, emergency gear, and blank checks.' [11]

In the article 'When White Women Cry: How White Women's Tears Oppress Women of Color' by Mamta Motwani Accapadi[12] in the section on The Intersection of Social Identities, she writes:

---

[11] https://www.nationalseedproject.org/Key-SEED-Texts/white-privilege-and-male-privilege?fbclid=IwY2xjawEmtr1leHRuA2FlbQIxMAABHd0E-2DYFhLyKGSXsYxGM4RbSm7x0xlmsQ3wrTFRz0dtmUBYIplS7nsbAw_aem_bUTvxkFH05uagH7jYy5LOw

[12] https://files.eric.ed.gov/fulltext/EJ899418.pdf

'All of our social identities inform and shape one another. One's identity as a woman is shaped by multiple factors in her life, including race, social class, sexual orientation, and so on. While sexism shapes the nature of womanhood, White womanhood looks very different than Asian American, Black, Indigenous, or Latina womanhood, because each woman's experience is shaped by the internal expectations and external perceptions of what it means to be a woman within each of these racial communities (Hernandez & Rehman, 2002; Anzaldua & Keating, 2002). Comprehensive historical research explicates this notion of racial identity informing gender identity (Daniels, 1997; Frankenberg, 1993; 1997). While White women have been depicted to be the foundation of purity, chastity, and virtue, Women of Color have historically been caricaturised by the negative stereotypes and the historical lower status position associated with their racial communities in American society (Hernandez & Rehman, 2002; Collins, 2000; Lorde, 1984; hooks, 1981). Additionally, as Palmer (1994) states, "the problem for White women is that their privilege is based on accepting the image of goodness, which is powerlessness" (p.170). This powerlessness informs the nature of White womanhood. Put in simple terms, male privilege positions the nature of womanhood, while White privilege through history positions a White woman's reality as the universal norm of womanhood, leaving a woman of color defined by two layers of oppression.

'As Dyer further elucidates, "White people set standards of humanity by which they are bound to succeed" (Dyer, 2005, p. 12). As a natural outcome, when there is conflict among women, the norms under which these conflicts are managed are based on White societal norms.'

My ex-friend was confronted by an image of middle-class Africans that did not fit her 'white saviour' mentality. She found Africans who were not poor, and it did not suit her stereotypes of narratives.

When I tried to understand the situation and try to explain the cultural context and the reason why she was insulting my family, I was brushed off and told that my concerns were insignificant. That's when it hit me: This friendship was no longer healthy. I knew that staying in this situation would only continue to harm my self-esteem. So, I made the difficult decision to distance myself from this person. It wasn't easy at first; I felt guilty and worried as we were very close and spent a lot of time together. But over time, I noticed how much lighter and happier I felt without that negativity in my life. This experience taught me that it's okay to let go of relationships that don't serve your well-being, even if it's hard.

Toxic Work Environment

Another situation where I had to set boundaries and eventually let go was in a workplace that had become toxic. At first, I loved my job and the people I worked with. It was a family-run concern, and they lacked professionalism. The rules changed at a whim. As much as I loved the work, the environment changed constantly. The wife became more demanding and the husband less supportive, and the office culture shifted to one of constant pressure and stress. It wasn't just about meeting deadlines anymore; there was unhealthy competition, favouritism, and a lack of appreciation for the hard work everyone was putting in. I began to dread going to work each day, and my mental and physical health started to suffer.

I tried to cope by staying positive and focusing on my tasks, but the negativity was overwhelming. It reached a point where I felt completely burnt out and unmotivated. I realised that no job was worth sacrificing my health and happiness. After a lot of thought, I decided to leave that job and start my own development consulting firm where I could thrive without the toxicity. The decision to leave was scary, but it was also incredibly liberating. Looking back, it was one of the best decisions I ever made for my well-being. It taught me the importance of prioritising my health and happiness over any external pressure.

Letting Go of a Harmful Relationship

Letting go of toxic relationships isn't limited to friendships or work environments; it also applies to romantic relationships. I had to walk away from my marriage. Although it was initially filled with love and excitement, it slowly became suffocating and harmful. The person I was with started showing controlling behaviour, questioning my every move, and making me feel guilty for spending time with friends or pursuing my own interests.

At first, I brushed these issues aside, thinking it was just a phase or something that would pass. But as the relationship progressed, the control became more intense, and I started to lose sight of who I was. I felt trapped, and my self-esteem plummeted. It was a difficult situation because part of me still cared deeply for this person, and I didn't want to cause them pain. However, I knew that staying in the relationship would only lead to more harm for both of us.

The realisation that I needed to end the relationship came after I discovered that my ex-husband was and had been unfaithful. It led to many heated arguments until I finally understood that this dynamic was toxic and unsustainable. I expressed the pain in the following note I made to myself:

January 13 and 24, 2020 – heartbreak

There is a wail that comes from the womb. It is a wail that only a woman betrayed can make. She cries out for what could have been and is no more. It only happens once, with the one you love. It is a howl into the wilderness. It is an ancient call to every woman who has gone before you and those who are to come.

In that moment, the world changes. It is never the same again. Yes, you can and will love again. Yes, you can and will forgive. Yes, you will live your best life. But that wail. That howl is only once. It signifies an end and a beginning.

'I cannot walk away. I must protect him. I love him. I have invested so much of myself in this.'

The confusion, anger, and rage, all cloaked in shame. I am ashamed. How do I face my children? How do I tell my loved ones? I am walking with this shame. Can they see it? I am this kickass professional, sashaying my way into business class lounges; I have anecdotes about Ministers and Heads of State and yet my life is falling apart. I have travelled to myriad countries, but I have never been to me.

'I do not want to be a statistic'. Do you know that the United Nations (UN) has the highest number of divorcees per capita? It is easier to be married. I do not want to be the angry feminist. I do not want to be bitter.

I will fight. Who is she? Has she bewitched him? There must be witchcraft involved! He is not himself. This is not us! This is not what we built!

And the compassion for her. I drowned in compassion. I saw myself in her. We met in an apartment in Braamfontein 13th floor, I think. A little bedsit. I asked her to come. They had been living together. He had asked her to clear out because I was coming. 'Oh, you're still married to her! The dragon. The controlling bitch whose family hates you! I thought you said she was mad.'

Well, the mad woman made dinner and was all civility. We even laughed together as we watched him squirm. But he wasn't squirming. He was celebrating. He had what he wanted. Two women to take care of his needs.

We lived together. We signed an agreement. In a bedsit, I slept on the bed with him, and she on the floor. We would even have sex. Shooshing each other and then having the guilt wash over me. Then I would think, 'Why am I guilty? I'm married.'

I signed an agreement with them. It was going to be a rational union. After all, I travelled. I was a consultant. I would come and go. In fact, she could be a helper. In many ways, it freed me.

And then, it became amusing. They would call me to arbitrate fights. I was called on to solve their squabbles.

I moved countries. I didn't have to do sharing in a country he could come to where we were. The first family.

But even that had to be sullied. My children had to witness the sexting. My son had to send me the transcript of the sexting in an email with the header 'I am sorry!' And in the body of the email, 'I could not send you the pictures!'

Tears streamed down my face as I read that email. I held my stomach as I took deep gulping breaths! Deep gulping breaths. And I asked myself why.

It wasn't fun anymore. I had hurt the people I loved most. I had inadvertently put them in harm's way. And suddenly, I had rage. I would fight for my children and for my marriage. First, I called them both – the agreement was voided. I raged and shouted, and I railed at them.

I was righteous in my anger. How could you? How could you take the innocence of my children?

His response, 'Oh, please, they are not innocent, with this unlimited Wi-Fi, do you think they have not seen porn? Oh, please, you're crazy. Your children are entitled. Your children are spoilt brats.

'You're crazy. Wadzi, you have tumours in the brain. After all, you're the one who is HIV positive, so who's the whore?'

I wailed! I hugged myself, and the wailing became silent. The tears rolled down my face. And I put on my body armour.

Was it over – no. Not yet. That was 2011. He promised he would not see her anymore. After all, she was a bitch who went out with married men. I was his whore, and she was his bitch.

I was a statistic. The research says it takes 7 attempts before a woman finally leaves – true. Ok, mine was cross-continental, involving Harare, Singapore, Beira, Rome, and Johannesburg. I'm extra like that.

Each time I went back, I had an excuse. Each time I believed the lies. Each time I told emotional Wadzi that she was being emotional. Rational Wadzi had this. We're not going to wail. It's going to be the modern story of polygamy. We're all going to live together.

Then it was, I think they're not together anymore. She's moved back to Zim and I'm with him now. I'm with him now. I win.

Then he was careless with his phone. And I picked it up. The dagger that was the message pierced my breastplate. They were still together. I shrivelled and died that day. But it was just another death.

I justified. I did my token outburst; it was a token now because the betrayal was becoming bigger than the rational thoughts. He soothed and, of course, comforted, and I slept in his arms that night.

The groundswell of revolt had started, though. Little Wadzi did not sleep. How many times must I put up with this? How many times? This is changing me. This is moving my goalposts. This goes against my values. Who Am I?

WHO AM I?

And the final straw. It was almost ludicrous in its absurdity. I was in a hotel room in Asmara. I had just finished a stimulating chat with him. Witty, fun and heartwarming. He was on a high. He had just graduated from his master's.

I just randomly scrolled through my contacts. Bored. I need to clear my contacts list. I do not interact with half of these people.

I stopped breathing. There was the picture he had sent me as he went to pick up his graduation certificate. The picture was taken by our son that morning. The picture was photoshopped with her – 'Congratulations, Rockie, we made it!'

We! Who is we? It was that question my daughter used to ask. 'Mum, do you agree with this? Mum, did you say this? Mum, is this a "we" thing?'

And my son's voice, 'We are no longer playing happy families, Mum. I do not want to play happy families anymore. It hurts too much. I do not want to lie.'

Who is we?! I chuckled as the tears rolled down my face. And his justification – I sent her the picture because I was happy. I just laughed and wrote back – 'Strike 3.' In baseball, you get 3 strikes then you're out.

I was out! I was done.

'Who is this person that I love?

How did I not see this?

Who are you?

Who was I married to?'

And the punch to the gut.

'Did you ever love me? Did you ever love me? Did you ever love me?'

Did you ever love me?

And then, I took my children. And I walked away. But the tentacles pull. The tentacles that try to believe that you did not love in vain. The tentacles that say – a 20-year investment of yourself, how could it end with nothing?

And as you slowly awaken, you ask, 'Who am I? Where did I go? Where am I?'

I am no longer. Your heart used to beat as one. You were cleaved together. The Bible says, 'Let no man put asunder.'

Mark 12:31 – The second is this: 'Love your neighbour as yourself. There is no commandment greater than these.'

'As you love yourself!'

Do I love Wadzi?

Who is Wadzi?

Where did Wadzi go?

It was one of the hardest decisions I've ever made, but I knew it was the right one. After ending the relationship, I took time to heal and reflect on what had happened. I learned a lot about myself, my boundaries, and the importance of maintaining my independence and self-worth in any relationship.

The Impact of Letting Go

Letting go of toxic situations is a form of self-care. It's about recognising when something or someone is not good for you and having the courage to walk away. Whether it's a toxic relationship, a negative work environment, or even a habit that's holding you back, letting go allows you to make room for better things in your life. It's not always an easy process – there might be guilt, fear, or even a sense of loss. But in the end, it's about choosing to value yourself and your peace of mind.

One of the most profound lessons I learned through these experiences is that it's okay to prioritise yourself. You deserve to be in environments and relationships that uplift you, not ones that drain you. It's okay to set boundaries and to say 'no' when something doesn't feel right. It's okay to let go, even when it's difficult. In doing so, you create space for positivity, growth, and healthier connections.

Lessons in Self-Respect and Self-Worth

Another key takeaway is that letting go doesn't mean you're giving up or failing; it means you're strong enough to choose what's best for you. It's about moving forward with your life in a way that aligns with your values and well-being. I've learned that by letting go of the toxic, I opened the door to more fulfilling and supportive relationships and situations. It's a continuous journey, but one that's worth taking for the sake of your peace and happiness.

In the end, letting go of toxic relationships and situations has taught me the importance of self-respect and the value of my own peace of mind. It's shown me that while change is hard, it's also necessary for growth and happiness. Surrounding yourself with positivity and support is crucial, and sometimes that means making the tough decision to walk away from what no longer serves you.

These experiences have also taught me to trust my instincts. Often, we know deep down when something isn't right for us, but fear or doubt holds us back from making a change. Learning to listen to that inner voice and act on it has been one of the most empowering lessons of my life. It's not about being selfish or uncaring; it's about recognising your worth and making choices that honour it.

Embracing New Beginnings

Letting go of toxic relationships and situations also opens the door to new beginnings. Once you've made the decision to leave behind what's harmful, you create space for new opportunities, relationships, and experiences that align with who you truly are. For me, this process has been incredibly liberating. It has allowed me to rediscover my passions, reconnect with people who genuinely care about me, and pursue paths that bring me joy and fulfilment.

It's important to remember that letting go is not a one-time event, but a continuous process. As we grow and evolve, we may find ourselves needing to reassess and let go of things that no longer serve us. This ongoing journey is about maintaining a healthy balance and ensuring that we are always moving towards a life that reflects our true selves and our highest good.

Letting go of toxic relationships and situations is an act of self-love. It's a declaration that you are worthy of respect, kindness, and happiness. It's about choosing to create a life that nourishes you rather than depletes you. And while the process can be challenging, the rewards are immeasurable. Through these experiences, I've learned that the most important relationship you can have is with yourself. By honouring that relationship and prioritising your well-being, you set the foundation for a life filled with peace, joy, and fulfilment.

On 19 March 2024, I wrote:

32 years ago, I heard the words "you are HIV-positive." It was 1992. I was 26 years old! I often wondered why I lived when so many others did not. With time, I learned that we all have our personal crises, and a lot of them are hidden from view. So, be your authentic self – be and do you, and the world will adjust. Exercise compassion for self and others. Give of yourself – your precious time because you can never gain time. Achieve your goals. Finish what you start. Walk away from things that do not serve you. Do not go where you are not celebrated and loved. Let go of toxic people and energy vampires. No is enough, no explanation is needed. Take a nap. You are not that important, so don't take yourself so seriously. Invest in art and anything that brings you joy. Surround yourself with beauty – in whatever way you define beauty. Live your best life. Never deplete yourself – emotionally, financially, physically, mentally, and spiritually for anyone. You are enough as you are. There is only one Wadzanai Valerie Garwe. For me, it is why I survived. Attend to your basic needs with compassion (ABC). And remember, what people call social norms change over time, so tradition changes. Make your own family traditions. You are a unique soul. Souls are fragile – handle with care!

#hivawarenessandprevention

CHAPTER 07

CHALLENGING CORE BELIEFS

Balancing Science, Religion, Astrology, and Mysticism

Throughout my life, I have been deeply curious about how the world works and what our place in it is. This curiosity led me to explore various ways of understanding life, ranging from the logical and rational to the spiritual and mystical. Over time, I've learned to balance science, religion, astrology, and mysticism, each offering its own unique perspective on the world.

Science

Science has always captivated me because it explains the world through facts and evidence. From a young age, I was fascinated by how science could provide answers to questions about how things work. Learning about the Earth's orbit, the growth of plants, and the fundamental laws of nature gave me clear, logical explanations that satisfied my curiosity.

Science taught me to ask questions, search for evidence, and think critically. I appreciated the reliability of scientific methods, which are based on experiments that can be repeated and observed. This approach made me feel confident in science as a tool for understanding the physical world around us.

However, as I grew older, I realised that science, despite its many strengths, doesn't have all the answers. While it can explain the 'how' of things – like how rainbows form or how our bodies function – it doesn't always address the 'why.' For example, science can describe what stars are made of, but it doesn't explain the sense of awe we feel when gazing at the night sky. This realisation led me to look beyond science to find other ways of understanding life's deeper questions.

Religion

As I searched for answers that science couldn't provide, I looked into religion. I am not religious. For many years, I was an agnostic, which means a person who believes that nothing is known or can be known of the existence or nature of God.

I had a conflicted relationship with religion. Religion offers guidance on profound questions about purpose, morality, and what happens after we die. It provides comfort, community, and a sense of connection to something larger than us.

In my life, religion has been a source of spiritual support, moral direction and questioning. It introduced me to the idea of a higher power, a force greater than any of us, that guides and watches over us. The teachings and values I found in religion helped me navigate life's challenges and make decisions that aligned with my beliefs. I was educated in a Catholic school, so I have elements of 'Catholic Guilt.'

However, the idea that a deity that is all-powerful, all-knowing, and loving could cause a child to be born HIV-positive conflicts with all I hold dear. Why would a deity allow an innocent child to be born to suffer?

These are the moments when the teachings of religion seemed to conflict with what I know from science. Science has made it possible for me to live a 'normal' life with the HIV virus within me. How did I get HIV? I was not promiscuous.

This created tension within me, but instead of feeling the need to choose between them, I began to see how both could coexist. I realised that science and religion address different aspects of life – science explains the physical world, while religion explores the spiritual and moral dimensions. By allowing both perspectives to coexist, I found a more holistic understanding of life.

I have also chosen a religion that I feel understands my conflicts. I am an animist. The *Oxford Dictionary* defines animism as '1. the attribution of a living soul to plants, inanimate objects, and natural phenomena. 2. the belief in a supernatural power that organises and animates the material universe.'

As an animist, I believe that all natural things, such as plants, animals, rocks, and thunder, have spirits and can influence human events: I gave up my agnosticism and became an animist.

Astrology

Astrology entered my life as people always asked, 'What month were you born?' I am a lion (Leo) in the zodiac and a horse in the Chinese zodiac based on my date and year of birth. I have very distinct Leo and horse traits. Astrology offered yet another way of understanding the world. Initially, I was sceptical of astrology because it didn't fit the logical, evidence-based approach I had learned from science. But as I explored it further, I discovered that astrology provided a different kind of insight, one more focused on personal reflection and understanding.

Astrology suggests that the positions of the stars and planets at the time of our birth can influence our personalities and lives. It's not about predicting the future with certainty, but rather about offering a framework for thinking about our strengths, challenges, and life's patterns.

For me, astrology became a tool for self-awareness. It helped me reflect on who I am and how I relate to others. I didn't view astrology as a science, but rather as a way to think about life's cycles and patterns. It provided comfort and insight, showing me that our lives move through phases and that understanding these phases can help us navigate them more effectively.

Mysticism

Mysticism added another layer to my understanding of life. Mysticism is about the direct, personal experience of the divine or the transcendent – something beyond the physical world that we can't easily explain. Mystical experiences are deeply personal and often leave us with a sense of awe and connection to something greater than ourselves.

Through mysticism, I explored practices like meditation and contemplation, which helped me connect with my inner self and with the universe in a spiritual way. These practices offered me peace and a sense of being part of something larger, even if I couldn't fully understand or explain it.

Mysticism taught me that not everything can be explained logically or scientifically. Some aspects of life are meant to be experienced and felt, rather than fully understood. This realisation allowed me to embrace the mysteries of life with a sense of wonder and acceptance.

Integrating Different Beliefs

Balancing science, religion, astrology, and mysticism has not always been easy. Each of these beliefs offers a different perspective, and sometimes they seem to contradict each other. However, I've found that instead of choosing one over the others, I can integrate them into a broader understanding of life.

Science gives me a solid foundation of knowledge about the physical world. It satisfies my curiosity about how things work and provides tools for critical thinking. Religion offers a moral framework and a sense of purpose, guiding me through life's challenges with spiritual wisdom. Astrology provides personal insights and a way to reflect on my life's journey, while mysticism connects me to the profound mysteries of existence.

By embracing these different perspectives, I've learned that life is multifaceted and that no single belief system has all the answers. Instead, each offers valuable insights that, when combined, create a richer, more nuanced understanding of the world and our place in it.

Personal Growth and Transformation

Exploring these diverse beliefs has been a journey of personal growth and transformation. It has taught me to be open-minded and to question my assumptions. I've learned to appreciate the complexity of life and to accept that some things are beyond human understanding.

This journey has also deepened my sense of empathy and connection with others. By exploring different ways of seeing the world, I've become more understanding of people who hold beliefs different from my own.

I've learned that we all seek meaning and understanding in our own ways, and that diversity of thought is something to be celebrated.

How These Beliefs Shaped My Worldview

Balancing different belief systems like science, religion, astrology, and mysticism wasn't an easy task. There were moments when these beliefs seemed to contradict each other, causing confusion and inner conflict. However, as I journeyed through life, I realised that each of these perspectives had something unique to offer.

Science provided me with a foundation of knowledge about the physical world. It helped me understand the mechanisms behind everyday phenomena, from the growth of a plant to the workings of the human body. This understanding was empowering; it gave me a sense of control and clarity in a world that often felt chaotic. Science taught me to value evidence, reason, and the importance of questioning what I didn't understand. It was a tool that allowed me to navigate the world with a clear mind and an analytical approach.

On the other hand, **religion** offered spiritual guidance and a moral framework that science couldn't provide. It gave me a sense of purpose and belonging, offering answers to the deeper questions of life – questions about existence, purpose, and the nature of good and evil. Religion was a source of comfort during difficult times, reminding me that I was part of something greater than myself. It taught me the importance of faith, morality, and community, grounding me in a sense of spiritual identity.

Astrology brought a different kind of insight. It provided a framework for introspection, helping me understand my own personality traits, emotions, and relationships. Astrology introduced me to the idea that life moves in cycles and that there is a certain rhythm to our experiences. This perspective encouraged me to look inward and explore the nuances of my emotions, behaviours, and interactions with others. It added a layer of self-awareness that complemented the rational understanding provided by science.

Then, there was **mysticism**, which opened the door to experiencing the divine or the transcendent in a deeply personal way. Mysticism was about embracing the mystery and wonder of existence, allowing me to experience life beyond what could be explained by science or understood through religious doctrine. It taught me to be open to the unknown and to accept that not everything could be neatly categorised or fully understood. Mysticism allowed me to connect with a deeper, more intuitive part of myself and the universe, fostering a sense of awe and interconnectedness.

Over time, I learned that these beliefs didn't have to exist in isolation. Instead, they could complement each other, offering a more holistic understanding of life. This blend of perspectives has shaped my worldview into one that is both grounded and open-minded. I've come to appreciate the strengths and limitations of each belief system, recognising that they each serve a purpose in my life.

Science taught me to appreciate the evidence and to ask questions, ensuring that I don't take things at face value. Religion showed me the value of faith and the importance of nurturing my spirit and maintaining a moral compass. Astrology gave me a tool for introspection, helping me to understand my own nature and the patterns in my life. Mysticism allowed me to embrace the unknown and to find peace in the mysteries of existence.

In my journaling of 7 July 2024, I reflected:

#conversationswithself Hermetic Philosophy is… "As within, so without, as above, so below, as the universe, so the soul."

And then Matthew 6:10, "Set the world right; Do what's best – as above, so below."

Wikipedia: "Quod est superius est sicut quod inferius, et quod inferius est sicut quod est superius."

That which is above is like to that which is below, and that which is below is like to that which is above.

In essence your heaven or your hell is in the here and now.

I'm always fascinated by how people ignore the philosophy of living in the moment.

To truly just be, one needs to be present. Meditation and prayer are about being in the present. In church, you are asked to feel the presence of God. Be still and know that I am God. The rest is noise. I have seen the majesty, the beauty, the complexity, the pain and the glory of going within.

My uncle is here, my mum's cousin, and the way we have similar tastes is mind-boggling. Peanut butter. Yesterday, my beautiful bonus daughter Zitgwai (meaning thankful) made us peanut soup – a Nigerian delicacy. My Sekuru and I were like kids in a candy store. Popcorn – we love it.

I have broken the matrix. Until you conquer your inner self, the rest is noise. You will travel the world seeking and return to the beginning – you!

When I am asked why am I so happy in spite of the turmoil. I'm happy because I have found myself. I have embraced myself. I love myself in my current form.

I'm fascinated by DNA. I sent a little blob of spittle, and the yield is fascinating. The DNA sample I sent determined that I am the perfect balance between warrior and worrier – highly adaptive and able to get the most out of stressful and not stressful situations. It determined I was Bantu, and my ancestry is Luhya, Yoruba, and Mende. Allergic to egg and lactose intolerant – all from a small blob of spit.

Science is validating what I'm experiencing in real time. I can understand my physical and mental capabilities and plan accordingly. I can fine-tune myself.

I am the miracle I am looking for. All the answers are within. You stand on the shoulders of your ancestors. Your DNA is the history of you!

Shae's eggs were in my Grandmother Soneni, my Mum Phillia and my granddaughter's eggs are in both of us.

This integrated approach to understanding the world has helped me stay curious, compassionate, and open to the complexities of life. It has allowed me to find balance and harmony within myself, as I continue to explore and integrate these diverse perspectives into my daily life. The balance of these beliefs has not only shaped my worldview but also allowed me to approach life with a deep sense of curiosity and wonder, always open to new insights and experiences.

CHAPTER 08

REFLECTING WISDOM

Reflecting on the Wisdom Gained from Your Life Experiences

Throughout life, we encounter a series of moments that profoundly shape our character, beliefs, and perspective. These experiences, whether filled with joy, sorrow, success, or failure, are the building blocks of our personal wisdom. Reflecting on them allows us to draw lessons that not only help us navigate our own lives but also offer valuable insights to others who may walk similar paths.

From childhood, our experiences begin to mould us. The lessons learned during these formative years often serve as the foundation for the wisdom we carry throughout life. For example, growing up in a supportive family might teach us the value of love and connection, while facing challenges at a young age can foster resilience and determination. These early experiences are crucial because they set the tone for how we approach life's ups and downs.

As we transition into adulthood, the stakes often feel higher, and the lessons learned can be more profound. Whether it's the experience of leaving home for the first time, starting a career, or forming meaningful relationships, each milestone offers its own set of challenges and rewards.

Reflecting on these moments helps us understand our growth, both personally and professionally. For instance, the courage it takes to leave a toxic environment teaches us about self-worth and the importance of prioritising our mental and emotional well-being.

The wisdom gained from relationships is another critical area of reflection. Interacting with others teaches us about empathy, communication, and the complexities of human connection. We learn to navigate differences, manage conflicts, and appreciate the beauty of diversity. Reflecting on our relationships, especially the challenging ones, can offer deep insights into our own behaviour and emotional needs. For instance, a difficult friendship might teach us about the importance of boundaries, while a loving relationship could reveal the power of unconditional support.

Career experiences also provide a wealth of wisdom. The professional journey is often filled with successes, failures, and everything in between. Each job, project, or interaction with colleagues contributes to our understanding of the working world and our place within it. Reflecting on these experiences allows us to refine our goals, recognise our strengths, and acknowledge areas for improvement. For example, a challenging project might teach us the importance of perseverance and teamwork, while a career setback could reveal the necessity of adaptability and resilience.

Life's most challenging moments, those marked by loss, failure, or adversity, often hold the deepest lessons. These experiences test our character and force us to confront our vulnerabilities. Reflecting on these tough times can be incredibly transformative. We might learn about the power of hope, the importance of patience, or the strength that lies in vulnerability. These lessons not only shape our future decisions but also enable us to support others who are going through similar struggles.

I struggled to write this memoir. I could not understand how I could put a lifetime of experiences into one book. The first chapter I wrote was called 'The Journey of a Tortured Mind,' and it went as follows:

I love writing; it has liberated me from pain. When I decided to write my memoirs, I thought I would give people a microcosm of my life. I am a big, beautiful, dark-skinned African woman turning 58 years old in August 2024. As I write this, I reflect on my journey through my tortured mind. I had lost myself between September 2019 and September 2021.

No, I did not lose myself. "Lost" is the wrong word.

I found myself.

I found myself in a psychiatric hospital called The Priory in Woking, Surrey, United Kingdom. I found myself in my spacious villa in Via Col di Nava 3, Monte Sacro, Rome, Italy, when I could barely get out of bed, keeping my room as dark as possible, and my pets – a husky named Loki (after the Norse God of mischief), a black chow chow named Sëga (which should actually be spelled Saga, as "Seeress" is a Goddess of poetry and history – even though he's male), and the cat, kitty kat aka Odin (the God of war and of the dead, ruling over Valhalla – "the hall of the slain." All Vikings who died in battle belonged to him. They were collected by his female handmaidens, the Valkyries. Odin was primarily worshipped by kings, warrior chieftains, and their men). Our cat Odin is female. As you can see, we are an eclectic family.

I found myself as I slowly allowed my suicidal ideation to recede, and I began to do things I enjoy, like taking a long bubble bath or walking my dogs. *I found myself when I downsized and moved from a five-bedroom villa to a two-bedroom home by the beach in Fregene, Rome.*

Who is Wadzi? In her innermost soul, Wadzi is a 21st-century nomad. She seeks experiences. As a long-term – 32-year – survivor of HIV, I feel that every moment is precious. I take loads of pictures to immortalise the moments because the pictures help me remember. I love hugging people and looking deeply into their eyes – because eyes are the windows to the soul. I don't like the word "survivor" because that implies the first level of the hierarchy of needs.

I don't just survive. I thrive! I bloom! I blossom!

I am like that flower that blooms through the crack in concrete. I bloom wherever I can. I bring sunshine and joy because this life is not a dress rehearsal. There's no second take or do-over. This is it, and boy, am I going to experience life. I pity people who have never experienced true love and true despair. I pity those who have never been through a life-changing event because then they never learn to truly savour the moment.

If you've never plumbed the depths of despair or reached the heights of ecstasy, then your life is bland and mediocre. I do not know how to lead an ordinary life. Drama, excitement, laughter, tears, joy, and pain abound in my life.

It's never mediocre.

I am uniquely made.

No one is like me.

I am a masterpiece in progress, not a work in progress. "Work" implies labour. A masterpiece is a passionately crafted piece of art.

My experiences have made me unique. I'm tenacious, and I fight for what I believe in. I've been called strong, but I dislike that word. Every African woman is strong. I am also vulnerable, and instead of "strong," I would say I am Zimbabwean. I'm like the French Peugeot 504 vehicle – indestructible, built to last.

*One of my favourite sayings is **"Life is about ebbing and flowing,"** which means letting things just be what they are without judgement. Don't force moments; let them evolve. People are always anxious and aiming for perfection. There is no such thing. I love a good party and will throw one at the drop of a hat. I can have a party of one, two, or many and still have a blast.*

*My second saying is **"exhale."** I know women who spend their lives breathing in and never exhaling because letting go is dangerous. My mother used to breathe in to stay slim. She only exhaled in her old age. Imagine a life where you keep your stomach in and control your breathing so that you conform to societal demands.*

*My third saying is **"There's only one of you, so do you and be authentically you – the world will adjust."***

*And the saying that saves me every day is **"Take it one breath at a time and one task at a time."** If opening your eyes is all you manage today, that's your task. I've been in a place where I didn't even want light. I wanted to die because I thought it would be better for the world but guess what – I'm a force of nature. My Italian colleagues and friends call me "una forza della natura."*

*Above all else, if you forget any of the sayings above, please remember this one: **"Always take care of your ABC – attend to your basic needs*** *with compassion."* Learn to exercise the compassion you use on your best friend. Life is too short to eat horrible food and drink bad wine.

I live my best, unapologetic life. I'd rather be mad, crazy and unconventional because conformity almost broke me! I'm huge – big heart, bear hugs, big feet, and just an overall ginormous heart filled with love. Infinite love for myself and for humanity.

This introduction showed me that I had attained equanimity and wisdom.

Wisdom comes from the quieter, everyday moments of life. The simple act of observing nature, engaging in a hobby, or spending time with loved ones can offer profound insights. Reflecting on these seemingly small experiences helps us appreciate the beauty of the present moment and recognise the value of mindfulness and gratitude. These moments teach us to slow down, savour life's pleasures, and find joy in simplicity.

As we accumulate wisdom from these varied experiences, it's essential to share it with others. Whether through mentorship, storytelling, or simply being a supportive presence, passing on our learned wisdom is a way to give back. By reflecting on our experiences and the lessons they've taught us, we can help guide others, offering them the benefit of our hindsight and insights.

Reflecting on wisdom also involves acknowledging the continuous nature of learning. No matter how much we've experienced, there is always more to learn and more wisdom to gain. This humility keeps us open to new ideas, perspectives, and experiences, enriching our lives further.

In the end, the wisdom gained from life's experiences is a treasure trove of knowledge that we carry with us. It shapes our actions, decisions, and interactions with the world. By regularly reflecting on this wisdom, we not only honour our past but also prepare ourselves for the future, equipped with the insights and understanding that can only come from a life fully lived.

Learning from Adversity

Adversity often becomes one of our greatest teachers, offering lessons that leave a lasting impact on our lives. When we face difficult situations, whether they are personal, professional, or emotional, we are pushed to our limits, and this forces us to tap into inner reserves of strength we might not have known existed. These experiences shape our character, teaching us resilience, empathy, and the importance of perseverance.

Facing Adversity: A Journey to Resilience

When life presents us with challenges, we are often compelled to dig deeper and find strength within ourselves. Adversity forces us to confront our fears, insecurities, and doubts, which can be daunting. However, it is through this confrontation that we discover our resilience the ability to bounce back, to keep moving forward even when faced by the seemingly insurmountable.

On 30 October 2023, I tied the leash of the dog around my waist, hopped on a bicycle, and ended up with a broken ankle.

I am a great believer in the Greek Gods because they are capricious, which the *Oxford Dictionary* defines as 'given to sudden and unaccountable changes of mood or behaviour.' I had just purchased the Rolls Royce of bicycle seats. I love innovators because they truly think through every possible issue. This seat was made for me. Più comodo in Italian – absolute comfort. This seat has springs and fits my ample girth. My bike was performing optimally. I love riding and I was channelling my 'white girl' with my beautiful Loki running beside me. Picture the moment. Optimal efficiency: the bike, the dog and I in total harmony.

It was a moment in time. In the next few minutes, I was on the ground and had popped my left ankle bone right out of its socket. Literally, the bone was to the left, and the rest of my foot limply hanging to my right. I'm the drama queen par excellence, except drama happens to and around me. When I'm in crisis, I generally become an observer. I kind of had an out-of-body experience where I was watching the reaction of everyone around me.

Italians are amazing people. Truly. I was helped by absolute strangers. An elderly lady stopped after I hailed her from my prone position in the middle of the road and quickly drove off to get help. A gentleman stopped, dragged me off the tarmac, put a cushion under my ankle, secured Loki and tied him against the park guardrails and all the while, he was chiding me and grumbling about how late he would be to his meeting. It would have been hilarious and farcical if I didn't have a bone sticking out of my ankle.

Everyone stopped.

No one took a video.

I was offered water, and every single person tried to make my situation better, all the while staring in horror at my ankle. The only reason I knew it was horrific was the expression on ordinary faces once they looked at the ankle.

In fact, I started waiting for the reactions, and no matter how stoic, there would be that 'pick my jaw up from the floor and ask the stupid question' moment. Mostly the question was, 'Did you break something?' And my knight, whose name escapes me right now, would look incredulously at the person and go, 'Are you blind? Her bone is sticking out of the socket! What do you think?' Honestly – farcical.

My knight bundled Loki into the back of his car, all the while grumbling at the inconvenience to his life. He was doing all this unsolicited. I gave him the keys to my home and showed him the gate key. I did not have my mobile phone. In fact, the bike ride was to collect my phone, which I had left on the back seat of a friend's car after an epic party on Saturday night. I couldn't call anyone because I had no numbers in my head. My little black book was on my table at home because I had taken my wallet, with my identity document, thank goodness, a bottle of water, and my house keys. I was going for a bike ride, after all.

On my knight's return, he found another kindly gentleman securing my bicycle to the nature park's guardrail. Fregene has these beautiful parks for humans and dogs, and I had my accident in between the nature park with a road separating it.

In the third stanza of my drama, my knight hands me back my keys and turns on the co-knight who is securing the bicycle and berates him for wanting to get my bicycle stolen. He then says, 'Give me that' – takes the bicycle and pops it into his trunk (boot for the English UK speakers). When he was asking me for my address, he had also asked if he could inform anyone. I told him about my retired next-door neighbours who should be home. Well, they weren't, and he was very annoyed at them. 'What could two elderly people possibly be doing away from home at lunchtime?' was his annoyed comment.

The ambulance arrived. Another comedic piece. Honestly, the health workers and first respondents have the most macabre humour. They are hilarious. The comedy of errors was about which hospital to take me to. The closest was Ostia Hospital along the seafront, 21 km away. The second option was Aurelia Hospital. As the first respondents argued with their colleague at home base, I snapped out of my observer status and told them that pain was setting in and my preference was Aurelia hospital. I had been to Ostia Hospital once to visit my nephew, and nah. It did not exude confidence, especially when it came to orthopaedics. No Italian has ever said to me the orthopaedic unit at Ostia Hospital – optimal. I had heard about Aurelia Hospital, though, and it's on our train route home.

I ended up in the fourth stanza of my personal drama – the emergency room. I must say that the bone sticking out of the socket got me immediate attention. I was whisked in. Prepped, then straight to the radiology unit, where the radiologist was going off shift and trying not to see me. Unfortunately, the patient before me was out in no time so he had to do my X-ray.

He was grumpy. While I waited, though, for radiology to get their act together, I was parked in the hallway and could again observe people's reactions to my ankle. The best was a nurse from Napoli (a city in Italy), Napolitana, who gave me the most honest 'oh shit, that must hurt' reaction. Her honesty was the best because everyone else tried to look as if it was normal to have a large African woman lying on a gurney smiling, while her ankle bone was sticking out of its socket. I either got the quick glance and then eyes forward, or the Buongiorno (good day) without asking how I was or the more informal 'Salve' (greetings)!

Remember, all this was happening in Italian. The sixth stanza (the fifth was the grumpy radiology person), I'm back in the emergency room ward awaiting the surgeon. The Napolitana nurse was attending to me and teaching me some choice swear words. Just a quick aside for non-Italians. Italy is made up of many tribes. Italians identify themselves by tribe. If you're from Rome, you're Romana, and this lady was from Napoli, hence Napolitana. That's the female if you're male, it would be Romano and Napolitano.

As I'm getting my lesson in Napolitana swear words, the surgeon rolls in and says, 'You've dislocated your ankle, and it's a clean dislocation, not a bad break.' In my non-medical head and Hollywood movies influenced mind, I thought that's fine – pop the bone back in the socket, and it will heal at home while I drink copious amounts of alcohol to dull the pain. Any excuse for gin and tonic! Isn't that every scene in a Hollywood movie – the hero takes a slug of alcohol while his/her mate pops the bone back and 'Bob's your Uncle.' I should have known from the medieval instruments of torture they wheeled in on a gurney that it was a little more complex. Then a lovely young anaesthesiologist said, 'I'm giving you some Valium while we pop your bone back,' and the next thing I know I was back in radiology.

At this point, Shae showed up looking frantic. I waved at her – clearly a little spaced out and high. 'Oh, it's just dislocated,' I said and floated off. When I next came too, I was in an orthopaedic ward in traction, and Shae was calmly explaining to me that no, I was not being discharged. It was not a simple dislocation – I needed an operation, and I was going to be in hospital for the foreseeable future. She did this very gently, patting and stroking my hand because both my children know I hate hospitals. She was also in Garwe girl commando mode.

We, the Garwe girls, are very good in crisis, courtesy of Phillia Garwe, our matriarch, who is a nurse. My mum goes still in crisis. She is that voice of reason as the world falls apart around her. She taught us to keep our heads in crisis. If you see a Garwe girl being dramatic and screaming, we're just having a moment, and it's not a crisis. In crisis, we baton down the hatches, and it's stiff upper lip all the way. Remember my admonitions about having your life in order.

On our shared health app, Shae was able to advise the nurses about my medication and the times it should be taken. She also emailed our health insurance provider and my supervisor. She went down to hospital administration and got the medical stuff all sorted out. As I said, channelling her Garwe girl. She also popped back home to bring all my medications, toilet bag, pyjamas, and computer so I could watch my Netflix. Go figure.

This happened on Monday, 30 October 2023. On Thursday, I had a bit of excitement because just before midnight, the nurses told me – no eating, you're going to surgery 'nil by mouth' – medical term. So, of course, that had me on high alert for most of my day until 15:00, when the nurse said, 'no surgery,' and I was starving. Down my emotions came, and we waited for surgery on Monday.

The health staff are amazing. Honestly, I could never be a nurse. Bedpans, bodily fluids, grumpy patients, call button going off at all hours, and just general mayhem.

I forgot, as the ambulance offloaded me, a critical care nurse came through the emergency ward and said, 'Well, today is just trauma day. We have a whole host of trauma patients,' and some bright spark behind him said, 'Well! It's a full moon!'

There you go. The full moon got me!

Health professionals are angels in human form. Okay, a few have a demon gene (fallen angels), but the majority are angels.

I am grateful for every health professional and first respondent.

As I recounted the way I fell off the bicycle, I had my therapist in stitches. We dissected how I got to this point as I had failed to listen to my intuition, disregarded my gut and gone against my instincts. Her observations were that the dog was just doing what a dog does. It stopped to defecate. It went with its instinct. I chose to tie the leash around my waist, which was irresponsible. I only had myself to blame. It also spoke to all the times in my life when I had allowed people's needs and wants to interfere with mine.

Experiencing a significant loss, such as the death of a loved one, or in my case, the loss of mobility, can be devastating. The grief and pain can feel overwhelming, making it difficult to see a way forward. Yet, over time, we learn to navigate this loss, finding new ways to honour the memory of the person or the use of the limb, we lost while continuing to live our lives. This process teaches us about the impermanence of life and the importance of cherishing our relationships while we have them.

In professional settings, adversity might come in the form of setbacks or failures. Perhaps we didn't get the promotion we worked so hard for, or a business venture didn't go as planned. These experiences can be discouraging, but they also offer valuable lessons. They teach us about the importance of perseverance, of not giving up even when the path ahead is uncertain. We learn to adapt, to find new strategies, and to keep pushing forward, building resilience along the way.

The Power of Empathy

Adversity also has a profound impact on our capacity for empathy. When we go through tough times ourselves, we become more compassionate toward others who are facing their struggles. We begin to understand that everyone carries their own burdens, and this awareness shapes how we interact with the people around us.

For example, someone who has experienced financial hardship may be more understanding and supportive of others in similar situations. They know firsthand the stress and anxiety that financial difficulties can bring, and this experience fosters a deeper connection with others going through the same thing. They become more willing to offer support, whether that's a listening ear, practical advice, or a helping hand.

This empathy extends beyond personal relationships. It influences how we engage with the world. We become more aware of the challenges faced by others, whether it's the struggles of marginalised communities, the impact of natural disasters on distant populations, or the daily difficulties faced by those living in poverty. Our own experiences with adversity help us to see the world through a lens of compassion and understanding, motivating us to be kinder, more patient, and more supportive.

Adversity as a Catalyst for Growth

Adversity is often a catalyst for personal growth. When we are pushed out of our comfort zones, we are forced to confront aspects of ourselves that we might prefer to avoid. This might include facing our fears, acknowledging our weaknesses, or letting go of preconceived notions. Through this process, we grow stronger, more self-aware, and more capable of handling future challenges.

As someone who has gone through a divorce, I have emerged from the experience with a deeper understanding of my own needs and boundaries in relationships. I have learnt what I want and don't want in a partner, and this clarity guides me in future relationships. This growth wasn't always easy or quick. It involved a lot of soul-searching, reflection, and sometimes, pain, but it ultimately led to a stronger sense of self.

The Importance of Perspective

One of the key lessons adversity teaches us is the importance of perspective. When we are in the midst of a difficult situation, it can be hard to see beyond the immediate pain or frustration. However, as time passes, we gain perspective on the experience, allowing us to see the bigger picture. We begin to understand how this challenge fits into the broader context of our lives and how it has contributed to our personal growth.

When I was forced to quit UNHCR, it felt like the end of the world, but with time, I realised that it was an opportunity to pursue a different career path, one that was more aligned with my passions and values. I was challenged by being self-employed, and it turned out to be one of the most lucrative things I have ever done. It helped me manage my finances, and we built a house for our young family.

This shift in perspective allows us to appreciate the role that adversity plays in guiding us toward new opportunities and experiences.

Building a Support System

Adversity also teaches us the importance of building and maintaining a strong support system. During tough times, the people around us, family, friends, and colleagues, can provide invaluable support, whether it's through offering advice, lending a listening ear, or simply being there for us. These relationships become a crucial part of our ability to overcome challenges, reminding us that we don't have to face adversity alone.

This experience of relying on others also teaches us about the importance of being there for others in their times of need. We learn that support is a two-way street, and that offering help to others not only strengthens our relationships but also enriches our own lives.

Adversity and Self-Discovery

Perhaps one of the most significant gifts of adversity is the opportunity for self-discovery. When we are faced with challenges, we are often forced to re-evaluate our priorities, values, and goals. We might discover new passions, strengths, or desires that we were previously unaware of. This process of self-discovery can be transformative, leading us to a deeper understanding of who we are and what we want out of life.

Being HIV-positive has given me a renewed commitment to taking care of my health, body, and mind. I have discovered a life-long passion for healthy living, mindfulness, good nutrition, and physical fitness that is a central part of my life moving forward. This self-discovery can lead to profound changes in how we live our lives, guiding us toward a path that is more authentic and fulfilling.

The Role of Adversity in Shaping Our Character

Adversity plays a crucial role in shaping our character. It tests our limits, reveals our strengths, and exposes our vulnerabilities. Through these experiences, we develop qualities such as patience, humility, and gratitude. We learn to appreciate the small victories, to find joy in the midst of hardship, and to remain hopeful even when the future is uncertain.

This character development is not always immediate. It often takes time to fully process and understand the impact of adversity on our lives. However, as we reflect on these experiences, we begin to see how they have shaped us into the people we are today. We recognise the resilience, empathy, and wisdom that have emerged from our struggles, and we carry these qualities with us as we move forward in life.

Adversity as a Teacher of Life's Greatest Lessons

In the end, adversity is one of life's greatest teachers. It offers us lessons that we might not have learned otherwise, lessons that shape our outlook on life and our interactions with others. While the experience of adversity is never easy, it is through these challenges that we gain the wisdom and strength to navigate the complexities of life with grace and courage.

As we continue on our journey, we carry the lessons of adversity with us, using them to guide our decisions, shape our relationships, and inspire our actions. We become more resilient, more compassionate, and more capable of facing whatever challenges life may bring.

Key Insights and How They Shaped Who You Are Today

Throughout life, we all gather pieces of wisdom from our experiences, shaping the way we see the world and interact with others. These key insights become the foundation of who we are, guiding our actions, decisions, and relationships. Reflecting on my own journey, there are several insights that have profoundly shaped the person I am today.

The Power of Optimism and Resilience

One of the earliest lessons I learned was the power of optimism and resilience. Growing up, I faced many challenges, some of which seemed overwhelming at the time. However, I realised that maintaining a positive outlook was crucial in navigating these difficult moments. Optimism helped me to see beyond the immediate struggles and to believe in a better future. It gave me the strength to push forward, even when the odds seemed stacked against me.

Resilience, on the other hand, taught me the importance of bouncing back from setbacks. Life is not without its share of disappointments, but I learned that it's not about avoiding failure it's about how we recover from it. This mindset has allowed me to face challenges head-on, knowing that each obstacle is an opportunity for growth and learning. These qualities have become cornerstones of my character, enabling me to approach life with courage and determination.

The Importance of Radical Acceptance

As I matured, I encountered situations that tested my ability to accept things as they were. Radical acceptance became a vital tool in my emotional toolkit, helping me to navigate relationships and life's unpredictability. I learned that there are aspects of life and people that I cannot change, and fighting against these realities only led to frustration and disappointment.

By embracing radical acceptance, I found a sense of peace and balance. It taught me to let go of the need to control everything and to appreciate life's complexities. This insight has greatly influenced my approach to relationships, allowing me to accept others for who they are without judgement or unrealistic expectations. It has also helped me to be more forgiving of myself, acknowledging my imperfections and understanding that they do not define my worth.

The Value of Setting Boundaries

Another significant insight was the importance of setting boundaries. In both personal and professional relationships, I realised that knowing where to draw the line was essential for maintaining my well-being.

I learned that boundaries are not about shutting others out but about protecting my energy and ensuring that I am treated with respect.

Setting boundaries taught me to prioritise my needs and to recognise when a situation or relationship was draining me rather than uplifting me. It was a difficult lesson, as it sometimes meant making tough decisions and letting go of toxic relationships. However, it ultimately empowered me to create a healthier, more balanced life. This insight has been crucial in helping me to navigate my interactions with others, ensuring that my relationships are based on mutual respect and understanding.

Embracing Compassion and Love

Compassion and love have been guiding principles in my life. I have come to understand that love, in its purest form, is about giving without expecting anything in return. This realisation has transformed my relationships, allowing me to connect with others on a deeper, more meaningful level.

Embracing compassion has also helped me to be kinder to myself. I have learnt to offer myself the same understanding and forgiveness that I extend to others. This insight has been instrumental in my journey towards self-compassion and has helped me to cultivate a more positive self-image.

Balancing Different Belief Systems

Balancing different belief systems has also played a significant role in shaping who I am today. Over the years, I have explored various philosophies, including science, religion, astrology, and mysticism. Each of these belief systems has offered valuable insights, and I have learned to integrate them into a coherent worldview. This balance has taught me the importance of being open-minded and curious. It has allowed me to approach life with a sense of wonder and to appreciate the diverse perspectives that exist in the world. This insight has not only enriched my understanding of the world but has also deepened my connection to others, as I have learned to respect and appreciate the beliefs that shape their lives.

The Courage to Speak My Truth

One of the most empowering insights I have gained is the importance of speaking my truth. Being honest and authentic has become a guiding principle in my life. I have learned that there is great strength in vulnerability and that sharing my experiences and perspectives can be both liberating and empowering. This insight has shaped my relationships, allowing me to communicate more openly and build deeper, more authentic connections with others. It has also influenced my personal growth, as speaking my truth has helped me to clarify my values and live a life that is true to who I am.

The Significance of Self-Discovery

Lastly, the journey of self-discovery has been a continuous process that has shaped my identity. Through introspection and reflection, I have gained a deeper understanding of my strengths, weaknesses, and desires.

This insight has guided me in making choices that align with my true self and has helped me to cultivate a sense of purpose and fulfilment.

Self-discovery has also taught me to embrace change and to be open to new experiences. It has allowed me to grow and evolve, becoming more aligned with my true self with each passing year. This insight has been a key factor in my personal development, enabling me to live a life that is authentic and meaningful.

CHAPTER 09

SPEAKING YOUR TRUTH

The Importance of Authenticity and Speaking Your Truth

Living an authentic life and speaking your truth are fundamental to achieving true fulfilment and meaning. Authenticity means being true to yourself and embracing your values, beliefs, and desires without trying to fit into the moulds created by others. It's about allowing your true self to shine through, free from the fear of judgement or rejection.

Living Authentically

Living authentically requires courage. It often involves making choices that go against societal expectations or the status quo. It means being honest with yourself about what you believe in, what you want out of life, and who you are at your core. This honesty extends to how you present yourself to the world, allowing your actions and decisions to align with your true self rather than being influenced by external pressures.

The journey to authenticity is not always easy. It can involve difficult decisions, such as leaving relationships that no longer serve you or pursuing a path that others might not understand. It may mean facing fears of being misunderstood, criticised, or even ostracised. However, the reward for living authentically is immense. It brings a deep sense of satisfaction, inner peace, and fulfilment, knowing that you are living a life true to who you are.

Consider the experience of someone who has always felt pressured to follow a traditional career path dictated by family expectations. My parents thought I was studying law and were shocked to discover that I had studied finance. I was not prepared to spend years in a job that didn't align with my passions or values, feeling unfulfilled and disconnected. Choosing to live authentically meant making the bold decision to pursue a different career, one that truly resonated with my interests and beliefs. This choice, though challenging because finance in Zimbabwe was in its infancy in 1989 when I graduated, led to a more meaningful and fulfilling life because it was in alignment with my true self.

The Power of Speaking Your Truth

Speaking your truth is an essential part of living authentically. It involves expressing your genuine thoughts, feelings, and beliefs, even when it's difficult. It means standing up for what you believe in, sharing your opinions, and being honest in your communication with others. Speaking your truth can be empowering.

It allows you to advocate for yourself, set boundaries, and make decisions that are true to your values. It also fosters deeper and more meaningful connections with others.

When you speak your truth, you invite others to see the real you, leading to relationships based on honesty and mutual respect.

When I was younger, I used to entertain the opinions of others over mine to avoid conflict. I would say yes to things that did not agree with my spirit instead of no. Over time, I felt frustrated and disconnected because

I was not being true to myself. Choosing to speak my truth about my HIV, mental illness, and divorce helped me provide my lived experience, and I was able to provide a different perspective in a discussion and stand up for my needs in a relationship. I can say no without an explanation and feel good about it. I feel more empowered and confident. This shift not only improved my sense of self but also enhanced my relationships, as others began to appreciate and respect my honesty. My daughter says I have no filter. Wadzi Unfiltered!

The shift from passive agreement to active expression of your truth not only enhances your personal well-being but also improves your relationships. As others witness your honesty and vulnerability, they are more likely to reciprocate with their own genuine selves, creating a foundation of respect and understanding. The courage to speak your truth can transform your interactions, leading to more authentic and fulfilling connections.

In essence, speaking your truth is about embracing who you are and communicating that with clarity and integrity. It is a vital step towards living a life that is true to your values and creating relationships that are grounded in honesty and mutual respect.

Challenges in Embracing Authenticity and Truth

In a world that often values conformity, the journey to authenticity and truth-telling can be challenging. There is a constant pressure to fit in, to meet societal norms, and to avoid standing out. The fear of rejection, criticism, or disapproval can make it difficult to be fully authentic and to speak your truth.

This challenge is compounded by the fact that living authentically and speaking your truth often involves vulnerability. It means exposing your true self to others, which can be daunting. There's a risk of being judged, misunderstood, or not accepted. However, it's important to remember that the courage to be vulnerable is also what allows for the deepest connections and the most meaningful growth.

One of the key steps in overcoming these challenges is developing self-awareness.

Understanding who you are, what you believe in, and what you want out of life is the foundation for living authentically. This self-awareness comes from introspection, reflection, and sometimes from making mistakes and learning from them. It involves asking yourself tough questions and being honest with the answers, even when they're uncomfortable.

Additionally, embracing authenticity means confronting societal expectations and the discomfort that comes with diverging from the norm. It involves standing firm in your values and beliefs, even when they are at odds with popular opinion. The process of aligning your actions with your true self requires both courage and resilience.

In navigating these challenges, it's also helpful to surround yourself with supportive individuals who encourage your authentic self-expression. Building a network of understanding friends and mentors can provide a safe space where you can explore and express your identity without fear.

Ultimately, embracing authenticity and truth is a journey of continual growth and self-discovery. It requires ongoing effort, self-compassion, and a commitment to living in alignment with your true self. Despite the difficulties, the rewards of deeper connections, personal fulfilment, and a more meaningful life are well worth the effort.

The Rewards of Authentic Living and Truth-Telling

Despite the challenges, the rewards of living authentically and speaking your truth are profound. When you live in alignment with your true self, you experience a greater sense of peace and fulfilment. You are no longer bound by the expectations of others or the need to conform. Instead, you create a life that is genuinely yours, one that reflects your values, beliefs, and desires.

Moreover, speaking your truth can lead to more meaningful and genuine relationships. When you are open and honest with others, you attract people who appreciate you for who you are. These relationships are based on mutual respect and understanding, rather than superficial appearances or false pretences.

Living authentically also empowers you to navigate life's challenges with confidence. When you know who you are and what you stand for, you are better equipped to make decisions, set boundaries, and face difficulties with resilience. You are less likely to be swayed by external pressures or to compromise your values for the sake of fitting in.

I lived a lie from the age of 26 until I turned 50. I did not disclose my HIV status to many people, including my parents. I was afraid of rejection, stigma, and questions. I had lived my life as if I were dying tomorrow.

In many ways, it was empowering because I had to set things right for my young family. In other ways it took away parts of me which could not share the inner turmoil.

On 6 August 2020, I wrote:

I was grieving for Wadzanai Valerie.

I lived my life in anticipation of my death. This is when Shae rolls her eyes and says, 'I guess we're going to hear about HIV again.' I always say, when I received my diagnosis, and, I do not know the exact date, but it was in 1992, I chose to live. The life I chose, though, was that I made a deal with God and the Universe. My deal was that I would live.

I would live on a clock.

I would cram my living into whatever time was left, and I would live on steroids; i.e., living an extreme life where everything is almost happening in fast forward.

But I also gave myself a limit. I had watched people around me die, so I figured I would live in 10-year cycles. So, I started running. First, I ran from Zimbabwe to Mozambique, and I hid. This is what shame does. My mother said to me, 'Wadzi, I have already mourned your death, I will not have to mourn you again!' I then came home. I like prodigal son/daughter stories, and I was the prodigal daughter returning home having redeemed myself as I was getting married. The next chapter of the redeemed, prodigal daughter was playing happy families. When playing happy families stopped working, I ran again. This time I ran to Rome to lick my wounds over a failing marriage, which was causing all sorts of schisms and ruptures in all my relationships. So, I got on a plane and ran as far away as I could. Then I decided to face my failing marriage, and I did all the ceremonial unconscious uncoupling things. Then, I said goodbye to Africa and took myself back to Rome. I spent my 50th birthday in a car with my son at the Beitbridge border post between South Africa and Zimbabwe, and I told him I never thought I would see my 50th birthday. I never thought I would see him grown.

My children were brought up to be fiercely independent almost to a fault. They have been latchkey[13] children for the most part, forced to grow up before their time and because of it, they are abrasive, and they do not understand 'playing happy families' because they associate playing happy families with being sad. There is a Dolly Parton song – 'I Don't Want to Play House.' That is the song I associate with my children. So, they challenge the happy families, and they challenge the status quo because they want reality, as painful as it may be, because they can understand reality.

And then, I did not die.

I still live each day as if it is my last, but before this, I really thought I would be dead by 50. And when I had to let go of a marriage that wasn't working, and really evaluate friendships and familial relationships and decide that okay, if I want to live, how do I choose to live.

I finally had to stop running away from Me.

I had to face the pain, the anger, the reality of living.

My depression was my final frontier. I had to face myself. I stopped running.

I have had to decide if I want to breathe and wake up tomorrow.

A person who has embraced their authenticity might find that they are more assertive in their career, more selective in their relationships, and

---

[13] 'Latchkey' refers to the key that children need to enter an empty house. Latchkey kids are kids between the ages of 5 and 13 who take care of themselves with no adult supervision before and after school on a regular basis.

more content in their daily life. They have a clear sense of purpose and direction, which guides their actions and decisions. This sense of clarity and alignment not only enhances their personal well-being but also inspires others around them to be true to themselves.

Practical Steps to Embrace Authenticity and Speak Your Truth

- **Self-Reflection**: Take time to reflect on your values, beliefs, and desires. Journaling, meditation, or simply spending time alone can help you gain clarity about who you are and what you want in life.

- **Courageous Conversations**: Practise speaking your truth in everyday situations. Start with small steps, like sharing your opinions more openly or setting boundaries in your relationships.

- **Embrace Vulnerability**: Recognise that vulnerability is a strength, not a weakness. Allow yourself to be seen and heard, even if it feels uncomfortable. Remember, it's through vulnerability that true connections are formed.

- **Let Go of Perfectionism**: Authenticity is not about being perfect; it's about being real. Embrace your imperfections and see them as part of what makes you unique and valuable.

- **Surround Yourself with Support**: Build a community of people who support and encourage your authenticity. These are the individuals who will appreciate you for who you are and will stand by you as you speak your truth.

- **Practise Self-Compassion**: Be kind to yourself as you navigate the journey to authenticity. There will be setbacks and challenges, but self-compassion will help you stay resilient and true to yourself.

- **Forgive Yourself**: Be kind to past versions of yourself that didn't know the things you know now. Hindsight is 20-20 vision. The decisions you made, the thoughts you had, and what you did and said were based on your reality at that time. Forgive yourself as you were doing your best to protect yourself.

Personal Stories of Courage and Honesty

Throughout my life, there have been several instances where I had to muster the courage to speak my truth and live authentically, despite the risks involved. These moments were not always easy, but they were crucial in shaping the person I am today.

One of the earliest instances where I learnt the importance of speaking my truth was during my time at the Dominican Convent School in Zimbabwe. Every day as Africans, we were in the minority. Every day we fought to be seen and heard. Our very being was under attack, from our hairstyles to our intellect, or lack thereof. I learnt to advocate for myself, and I became an activist for others who were afraid to speak. I have never and will never understand injustice based on systematic racism or a system that dehumanises others.

The experiences at school were deeply painful and left me feeling invalidated. They were also pivotal moments in my life. My parents, though disheartened by the constant need to have conversations about race, encouraged me to stay true to myself and my abilities. They assured me that one day, my talent and hard work would be acknowledged. This lesson in resilience and self-belief stayed with me and became a cornerstone of my journey towards authenticity.

Another significant moment came in my adulthood when I found myself in a toxic marriage. The relationship was draining and destructive, yet I stayed because I feared the stigma of divorce and the uncertainty of starting over. However, as time went on, I realised that staying in the marriage was causing me to betray myself. I was living a life that was not true to who I was, and it was taking a toll on my mental and emotional well-being.

The decision to leave the marriage was one of the hardest decisions I have ever made. It required me to confront my fears and take a stand for my own happiness and well-being. Leaving meant facing judgement and criticism from others, but it also meant reclaiming my life and living authentically. This experience taught me the power of speaking my truth, even when it's difficult, and the importance of prioritising my own needs and happiness.

Speaking my truth also played a crucial role in my professional life. After I suffered a mental and physical breakdown having been held hostage, after recovery, I tried to apply for a post for promotion. After passing the written test, the feedback I received was that I had done well in the interview. I did not get the job. My supervisor then said I was not considered for the promotion because 'management could not trust me.' They were afraid that any stress would result in a relapse.

The audacity of management. Firstly, I had been declared fully competent by a medical doctor to return to work. Secondly, it was an invasion of my privacy. I realised that I was working in an environment that was not aligned with my values. The division's practices and policies conflicted with my beliefs, and I felt increasingly uncomfortable continuing in my role. However, the prospect of leaving a stable job and venturing into the unknown was daunting.

After much reflection, I realised that staying in the job would mean compromising my integrity and living inauthentically. I made the difficult decision to find an alternative post away from the toxicity. This decision was a turning point in my life, as it allowed me to pursue work that was more aligned with my values and passions. It also reinforced the importance of speaking my truth and living in a way that is true to who I am.

Perhaps one of the most profound moments of truth-telling in my life came when I publicly disclosed my HIV-positive status at the age of 50. For years, I had kept this part of my life hidden, fearing the stigma and discrimination that often accompanies such a disclosure. However, as I grew older, I realised that living in secrecy was preventing me from fully embracing my life and my story.

The decision to speak my truth and share my status with the world was both terrifying and liberating. It required immense courage to confront the fear of judgement and rejection, but it also allowed me to live more authentically. By sharing my story, I was able to connect with others who were going through similar experiences and to advocate for greater understanding and compassion towards those living with HIV. This experience taught me that speaking your truth can be a powerful act of self-liberation and a means of creating positive change in the world.

These experiences have taught me that authenticity and truth-telling are not just personal choices but acts of courage that have the power to inspire others. By living authentically and speaking my truth, I have been able to create a life that is true to who I am and to build deeper, more meaningful connections with others. It has also allowed me to navigate life's challenges with greater resilience and to find peace and fulfilment in being true to myself.

My favourite expression is, 'Be you and do you authentically – the world will adjust!'

CONCLUSION

FINAL REFLECTION

As I reflect on this journey, I am reminded of the transformative power of resilience, compassion, and the unwavering belief in the goodness of life. Through the stories and experiences shared in this book, I have revisited the moments that have shaped me, the lessons that have guided me, and the values that have anchored me. Each chapter represents not just a phase of my life but a fundamental piece of who I am, a person who has learned to navigate the complexities of life with grace, courage, and an open heart.

The path I've walked has been filled with both light and shadows. The early lessons in resilience, drawn from my childhood in Zimbabwe, instilled in me a sense of determination that has carried me through life's inevitable challenges. The experiences at the Dominican Convent School, where I first encountered the harsh reality of racial bias, taught me to maintain my dignity and self-worth even in the face of injustice. These early experiences were not just formative they became the foundation of my belief in the importance of perseverance and the inner strength needed to thrive in an often challenging world.

At my core, I am a believer in the potential for growth and healing. I have come to understand that life's challenges are not merely obstacles to overcome but opportunities for deeper self-awareness and connection with others. My journey has taught me that embracing radical love, setting boundaries, and practising self-compassion are not just acts of kindness to oneself, but essential practices for living a fulfilled and authentic life. Whether it was learning to accept myself with compassion after a significant mistake at work or discovering the importance of setting boundaries to protect my emotional well-being, each lesson has added depth to my understanding of what it means to live authentically.

The core values that have emerged through these experiences are resilience, compassion, integrity, and authenticity. They are the pillars upon which I stand. They are the guiding lights that have led me through darkness and have illuminated the path ahead. Resilience has been my anchor, allowing me to weather life's storms with a sense of hope and determination. Compassion, both for myself and others, has opened my heart to a deeper level of understanding and empathy, enabling me to connect with others in meaningful ways. Integrity has kept me grounded in my principles, ensuring that my actions are always aligned with my beliefs. Authenticity has empowered me to live my truth, even when it meant defying societal expectations or walking a path less travelled.

In embracing these values, I have found a deeper understanding of who I am and the purpose I wish to fulfil. This journey has not just been about surviving but about thriving and finding joy and meaning in each moment, about learning to appreciate the beauty of life's imperfections, and about recognising the strength that comes from vulnerability. The stories in this book are not just my stories; they are reflections of universal truths that resonate with anyone who has ever faced adversity, grappled with self-doubt, or sought to live a life of purpose and meaning.

This book is a testament to the power of storytelling, not just as a way to reflect on the past, but as a means of offering hope and inspiration to others. It is my hope that by sharing these experiences, others may find the courage to embrace their own journey with an open heart and a resilient spirit. In these pages, I have laid bare my fears, my triumphs, and my growth, not just to share my story but to create a space where others can see themselves and their own potential for growth and transformation.

In conclusion, this journey has been one of self-discovery, healing, and growth. It has been about finding my voice, speaking my truth, and standing firm in my values. I am deeply grateful for the lessons learnt, the love received, and the strength gained along the way. As I move forward, I do so with a renewed sense of purpose, grounded in the knowledge that I am enough just as I am, and that my story – like everyone's – matters. I carry with me the understanding that life is not about avoiding the storms but about learning to dance in the rain. And in that dance, I have found a rhythm that is uniquely mine, one that celebrates the fullness of life in all its beauty and complexity.

Attend to your Basic Needs with Compassion (ABC)!

ABOUT THE AUTHOR

Wadzanai Valerie Garwe

Wadzanai Valerie Garwe is a mother of 2, an author, an HIV and mental health activist, an executive coach, a mentor, an experiential teacher and learner, a long-term survivor of HIV (32 years) and a firm believer in the power of economic empowerment. The name Wadzanai means reconcile, or live in harmony, in Shona. Wadzanai was born in Zimbabwe where she did all her primary and high school education, and she did her undergraduate and postgraduate degrees in the United States. Professionally, Wadzanai is an economist, who studied finance and community economic development. She works in international development, has run a freelance development consulting business, and a family agricultural concern of 180 hectares. She is a coach and mentor, centering her coaching on workplace toxicity. She started a Trust Organisation, Edmund Garwe Trust, in memory of her late father, who believed that education was the means to financial, mental and physical freedom. The Trust provides scholarships to child- headed households, especially those whose parents died of AIDS (Mukondombera). The book 'Beyond and Behind the Faces of HIV and AIDS' is available on Amazon and major bookstores and libraries worldwide. She is a co-facilitator of a platform called 'African Conversations with Self' (ACwS), which that is collecting a video and audio anthology of lived experiences of post-colonial Africa. She believes in the power of conversations and the power of lived experiences. She has lived and worked in many places, and her passion is to ensure that she lives her best life, and contributes towards making the amazing world we live in a wondrous adventure of growth and self-discovery. Wadzanai currently lives in Italy.

Get hold of Wadzanai via the following platforms:

Email: wadzanaigarwe@gmail.com
LinkedIn: www.linkedin.com/in/wadzanai-garwe
Twitter: @wadzigarwe
Instagram: @wadzanaigarwe
Facebook: https://www.facebook.com/wadzanaigarwe

Amazon: https://www.amazon.com/author/wadzanaivaleriegarwe

Subscribe to African Conversations with Self
Patreon: https://www.patreon.com/africanconversationswithself

Follow, like and comment on our podcast on Apple and Spotify:
https://podcasts.apple.com/.../conversati.../id1592075182
https://open.spotify.com/episode/4v50cnBlhz4qgX4tJ54v9b...

Stepping Into Wadzi – Lessons from My Life: Call to Action

Stepping into Wadzi – Lessons from My Life is a masterclass in healing. Everyone on earth was born unique and perfect. Life then slowly chips away at the perfection leaving a broken soul. Souls are fragile and need to be handled with care. This book is a how-to that calls to any woman of colour, who has navigated micro-aggressions, sexism, racism, and many other stereotypes to heal their inner and outer child and step into their higher self.

Wadzanai has had the breakdown and, burnout, reached a CD4 count of four which means she had full- blown AIDS, and lived a full life as a professional economist, mother, sister, friend, wife, divorcee, and all-around phenomenal woman.

Once you read this book start working on your healing.

Get the therapy you need.

Follow inspirational thought leaders.

Start journaling your healing.

Take the first step to living your best life and realize your dream.

Follow Wadzi on LinkedIn, Facebook, and Instagram.

Share your thoughts with her on these platforms.

Become part of Wadzi's tribe that walks away from toxicity and steps into self-actualization and living a fulfilled life.

www.ingramcontent.com/pod-product-compliance
Lightning Source LLC
Chambersburg PA
CBHW071744120626
46550CB00002B/655

* 9 7 8 1 9 6 6 7 9 8 1 1 8 *